Above: Before the paving of modern-day roads in Florida, travel was often on narrow sandy paths.

Left: Before modern roads, navigable rivers were often used for transportation. The resort of Silver Springs was reached from the Ocklawaha River by traveling up the mouth of the Silver River by steamboat. The resort became a popular destination for tourists following the Civil War and remained so into the next century. Among the guests who came to the resort were Robert E. Lee, Ulysses S. Grant, Mary Todd Lincoln, Harriet Beecher Stowe, and Calvin Coolidge.

Front Cover:
Historic Whitehall was a 75-room, 60,000-square foot winter home for Henry Flagler and is now the home of the Flagler Museum. Flagler was a partner of John D. Rockefeller in Standard Oil and used his substantial wealth to pursue a dream of a railroad system connecting tourist resorts in Florida. The home was built as a gift for his then wife, Mary Lily Kenan. At the age of 83, Flagler fell down the steps of Whitehall and never recovered.

TABLE OF CONTENTS

SITE LIST

INTRODUCTION

In the minds of many, Florida is "new." While early Native Americans apparently reached Florida ten to twelve thousand years ago, the presence of humans and their ancestors can be traced much longer in the so-called "cradles of civilization:" Mesopotamia, China, India, and Africa.

Relatively little is known of these earliest Floridians, largely because they had no known written language. Unlike the Egyptians, their pyramids were shell and burial mounds; otherwise what they left behind was their handiworks, from which today's humans try to distinguish and comprehend their cultures.

The history of Florida documented in writing begins with visits by the European explorers and the subsequent European invasion. This history is roughly 500 years old. Compared to the Middle East, this is "new" history. However, that does not mean that the history is not plentiful.

Unlike New England, three colonial powers contested for the lands that include the present Sunshine State. America's "first" city is not Boston or New York, but St. Augustine. Although Florida's role in the American Revolution could be declared non-existent, it was occupied by Europeans, Africans, and their descendants (albeit sparsely) longer than any other area of the U.S. Florida was a possession of two countries: Spain and England. It has had several capitols, been a U.S. territory, a Confederate state, undergone Reconstruction, struggled as a frontier, seen its own "Indian" wars, played a role in the Spanish American War and Cuban history, and exploded into the fastest-growing state in the country. Along the way, it has struggled with civil rights, fought to preserve its environment, sent men to the Moon, and survived the Great Depression.

There are thousands of historical sites in Florida. To include all of these in one book would not be possible. The authors have provided a sort of "thumb-nail" sketch of each of Florida's historical periods plus some special topics, like Florida's role in Hollywood and writers and artists who have lived here. With each historical period or topic, sites have been selected that are either easily accessible or best illustrate the history.

USING THIS BOOK

Each site (or field trip) contacts included in this book are listed in Appendix A. This includes a mailing address, usually a website, and often a phone number. Before visiting the sites in the book, it is recommended the visitor check hours of operations. Some of the sites are open almost round-the-clock. Others are only open a few days a week. Still others may have limited or restricted access. Of course, operating hours can change, and unfortunately some of the institutions may have to close their doors for lack of funding.

THE REAL TOURIST STATE

Forty million years ago, according to current geological research, Florida was not part of the continental U.S. or North America. It was a submerged continental shelf off Africa. Over a period of 10 to 15 million years, Florida traveled underwater toward North America via "continental drift," the very slow movement of land on colossal geological structures below, referred to as tectonic plates. By 25 million years ago, Florida was pretty much in its current location, with the Georgia Channel separating it from its current attachment to the U.S. "Sand and silt cascaded off the continent onto Florida, and Florida became dry land. Today, Florida is a layer cake with a foundation of African rocks, a core of limestone, and an icing of sand." (*Florida's Fabulous Natural Places,* 1999, Ohr, World Publications, 1999)

BEFORE MAN

Once upon a time, Florida was a submerged continental shelf migrating from off the coast of Africa to its current position. During the 5% of its existence above water, Florida has been home to some strange creatures either extinct or unknown in present times. These have included at various periods such things as very large armadillos, camels, giant hedgehogs, mastodons, Oligocene horses, peccaries, rhinoceroses, and saber-tooth tigers. Some of these species were still present in Florida when the earliest Native Americans arrived. Current theory holds that the gatherers and hunters arrived perhaps 12,000 years ago and proceeded to hunt down whatever game they could kill, speeding the demise of many of these exotic creatures.

No one knows for sure when humankind reached the North or South American continents. Current belief among anthropologists is that humans crossed onto the North American continent over formerly submerged land between Siberia and Alaska; this occurred, they believe, during the last Ice Age, over 12,000 years ago. There is growing evidence that some humans may have arrived earlier; however, they left behind few artifacts, and their presence was small and spotty.

The earliest evidence of sustained Indian presence in Florida is from roughly 12,000 years ago. The lives of these humans are not written down on paper but exist in the tools they made, how they appear to have fished and hunted, and how they buried their dead.

WILD FLORIDA

The land into which Paleoindians entered can only be envisioned through an imaginative mind. Modern Floridians are used to buying tools down at the hardware store, but ancient humans made their own tools from bones, rock, shell, shrubs, and trees. To survive they had to catch, kill, or grow what they ate in a dangerous wilderness.

The only shelters were what the natives built, sometimes on mounds, for Florida generally lacked caves. What these ancient humans felt or thought when they looked up at the stars at night and saw a meteor or the moon, no one knows. Certainly, like humans everywhere, they procreated during their lives, thus presumably loved and lusted, to the extent that there were somewhere between 150,000 and 300,000 Native Americans in Florida when the Europeans arrived.

⋏ *Tocobaga Fishing by Hermann Trappman.*

EARLY NATIVE AMERICAN EPOCHS

Archaeologists have divided periods in Florida's early history of cultures based primarily on changes in tools and spear points. They have also described various cultures of native peoples who shared similar ways of making implements or ways of obtaining their food. These rough timelines and periods are often used and so it is helpful to understand what they meant.

TIME	PERIOD	
10000 – 7500 B.C.	Paleoindian	Hunting, foraging
7500 – 5000 B.C.	Early Archaic	Initial settlements
5000 – 3000 B.C.	Middle Archaic	Tool variety
3000 – 500 B.C.	Late Archaic	Tempered pottery
500 B.C. – 1000 A.D.	Woodland	Pottery
1000 – 1600	Mississippian	Mounds and corn
1600 – 1710	Acculturative	Spanish influence

EARLY NATIVE AMERICANS

The people who greeted the first Spanish explorers were a scattered lot, with perhaps 100 different names. Often they were not formally organized but merely shared a language. They probably lacked chiefs or kings until relatively late in their histories. They were not Seminoles. The Seminoles are descendants of Lower Creek Indians from Georgia, who moved into Florida in the late 1700s after the original tribes died out; those Lower Creeks eventually were joined by Upper Creek refugees from Alabama in the 1810s. Three of the names we use today to describe the 100 or so language groups that the Europeans first confronted are the Apalachee, Calusa, and Timucuan.

▲ *The Calusa built a 2.5-mile canal across Pine Island into Matlacha Pass.*

▲ *This Timucuan totem pole of a Great Horned Owl was dredged out of the St.Johns River near DeLand. It was probably made around 1350.*

APALACHEE

The land of the Apalachee was between the Aucilla and Ochlockonee rivers in Northwest Florida. This area appears to be the oldest land continually inhabited by Native Americans in Florida, including Paleoindians, who preceded the Apalachee. The Apalachee farmed and lived in towns, including what is present-day Tallahassee. The Apalachee, who allied with the Spanish, may have numbered 50,000 when the Spanish reached the Americas.

CALUSA

Coastal people of South Florida, the Calusa lived on shell mounds and prospered by harvesting fish and shellfish. "Fierce" is a word frequently over-used to describe the Calusa, who resisted Spanish assimilation for two centuries. For the Catholic Spaniards, the Calusa were true pagans, believing in human sacrifice and sometimes practicing brother-sister marriage, like the early rulers of Egypt. When Ponce de Leon and early Spanish explorers reached San Carlos Bay between Fort Myers and Sanibel Island, Calos, the leader of the Calusa, conducted aggressive attacks repelling the invaders.

TIMUCUAN

Timucuan-speaking people were widespread in the northern portion of Florida, but not the Panhandle, where the Apalachee lived. By the 1730s, most Timucuan were dead and gone (due to exposure to European diseases and conflicts with their Native American rivals), although a few survived a little longer. The Timucuan were the largest Native America group when the Spanish landed in Florida, numbering perhaps as many as 150,000.

CALUSA HERITAGE TRAIL (Lee County)

Visitors to the Randell Research Center can tour the Calusa Heritage Trail, a 3,700-foot interpretive walkway that leads visitors through the mounds, canals, and other features of the Pineland archaeological site. Museum-quality interpretive signs along the improved trail provide visitors with detailed information regarding the Calusa Indians who inhabited the Pineland site, their culture and environment, and the history of Southwest Florida after the Calusa left. The trail also features observation platforms atop the site's tallest shell mound, in addition to trail side benches and a boardwalk and bridge over low-lying areas. Parking is available inside the main gate to the Randell Research Center at 13810 Waterfront Drive. Public rest rooms and picnic facilities are also provided. The trail is located in Pineland at 13810 Waterfront Drive. From I-75, exit west on SR-78 and proceed to Pine Island. Once on Pine Island, turn north on the sole north-south road. After about 3 miles, turn left on Pine Island Road and follow it to the waterfront. The facility is presently open daily and has regularly scheduled guided tours part of the year. As this may change, visitors may wish to check with the website in Appendix A.

CRYSTAL RIVER ARCHAEOLOGICAL STATE PARK (Citrus County)

Native Americans inhabited this area from approximately 10,000 to 500 years ago; evidence of their presence remains in six mounds that can be visited on a .75-mile interpretative trail. From a viewing platform, Temple Mound A overlooks Crystal River and can be ascended via a stairway. The site is a National Historic Landmark, and the visitor's center has both a video display and exhibits. Two miles north of Crystal River on US-19, turn west on State Park Street and follow it until it enters the park.

▽ *Along the coastlines of the southern half of Florida, mounds were generally built above mangroves.*

EMERSON POINT PRESERVE
(Manatee County)

Emerson Point lies in the southern mouth of Tampa Bay. Surely early Spanish explorers passed it and perhaps encountered the Native Americans living on it. This county preserve includes what is said to be the largest remaining mound on the West Coast and a number of middens (refuse heaps). In one part of the preserve, a Native American village is said to have existed for 1,000 to 1,600 years; interpretive signs help carry the visitor back in time. In addition, Emerson Point Preserve is a wonderful place to visit. There are paths winding along mangroves with scenic overlooks of Tampa Bay and a tall observation tower from which the area can be observed, including the tiny little cars in the distance zipping up and down the Sunshine Skyway Bridge. From Business 41 in Palmetto, turn west on 10th Street West and follow the signs to the park at 5801-17th Street West.

FLORIDA NATIVE-AMERICAN HERITAGE TRAIL (Statewide)

This concept trail includes roughly 100 locations related to Florida's Native-American heritage. These sites are from both the early Native American period and the times of the Seminoles. Many of the sites are within this book. A wonderful brochure describing all the sites is available from the Division of Historical Resources.

INDIAN TEMPLE MOUND MUSEUM
(Okaloosa County)

Preservationists everywhere probably owe it to the Gulf Coast City of Fort Walton Beach for preserving this site along with more than 6,000 relics from early Native Americans. In 1962, this was the first municipally owned and operated museum in Florida. Temple Mound is large, and said by the city website to be probably the largest mound on the Gulf Coast. The city says more than 500,000 baskets of earth and shells were necessary to create this mound. The museum also has exhibits from settler times, the Civil War, and periods of European explorations. Fort Walton Beach lies beside Eglin Air Force Base in the Florida Panhandle. From I-10, as a reference point, take SR-85 south until it meets US-98. The museum is nearby.

JONATHAN DICKINSON STATE PARK
(Martin County)

Thousands of visitors each year explore more than a dozen natural communities within Jonathan Dickinson, however few are aware of Dickinson's daring journey through eastern Florida more than 300 years ago. Shipwrecked off Jupiter Island in 1696, Dickinson and 23 surviving Quakers wandered hundreds of miles in the vast unwelcoming Florida wilderness. Encountering hostile indigenous tribes along the months-long journey northward, survivors were clubbed and stoned. Lives were lost to yellow fever, exhaustion, and extreme conditions, before a rescue party led by Spanish soldiers accompanied by other Native Americans guided the wayward group north to St. Augustine. Dickinson's detailed diary of survival provides modern scholars with some of the earliest accounts of Florida, its native inhabitants and their customs. Jonathan Dickinson State Park is off US-1 just south of Hobe Sound in Southeast Florida.

LAKE JACKSON MOUNDS ARCHAEOLOGICAL STATE PARK
(Leon County)

During a visit in the late 1990s, the lake for which the site is named was a dry bed, filled with magnificent fields of yellow flowers. On a return visit in 2007, a sea-like lake stretched into the distance. Such contrasts are routine and caused by both drought and sinkhole activities. Within the state park are six mound remnants. Human remains, tools, and decorative items are among those excavated from the site. Between 1825 and 1860, the site was part of a plantation belonging to Colonel Robert Butler, Florida's first Surveyor General. From I-10 in Tallahassee, exit north on US-27. Within two miles or less, turn east on Crowder Road, then south on Indian Mounds Road, where there is parking.

LECHWORTH-LOVE MOUNDS ARCHAEOLOGICAL STATE PARK
(Jefferson County)

Named for the family providing the land to the state, the park contains a mound complex 1,000 to 1,700 years old. At least 15 mounds existed at the park site at some point within recent history, however most were destroyed by agricultural use before state acquisition. At 46 feet in height, the mound immediately visible is said to be the tallest surviving in Florida; it is approximately 300 feet wide. Like all such mounds in Florida, it seems to provide a good place for trees to grow, including pines, oak, and magnolias. From I-10, exit on US-90 east and turn south on Sunray Road and go approximately 14 miles. The site is at the end of the road.

MADIRA BICKEL MOUND STATE ARCHAEOLOGICAL SITE (Manatee County)

Hernando de Soto may have visited the site, which was perhaps inhabited for 2,000 years. A single mound remains on a sliver of land. Like all the archeological sites, one must stand atop the mound to imagine what life must been like before the conquistadors came. From I-275 south of the Sunshine Skyway Bridge, exit south on US-19. Shortly, Bayshore Drive will appear on the west side of the road at the second sign announcing the site. Turn west on Bayshore and make a jog onto 57th Street. The site will be evident.

⚲ *An old photo of a man climbing the Turtle Mound shell midden. This famous shell mound is located seven miles south of New Smyrna Beach and covers 16 acres.*

MOUND KEY STATE ARCHAEOLOGICAL PARK (Lee County)

The Calusa town of Calos (corrupted by the Spanish into Carlos) with a population of perhaps 1,000 was once located on Mound Key, an island of about 225 acres. From Calos, Calusa kings ruled from perhaps 600 A. D. until the Spanish invasion. Calusa kings dwelled atop what is presently identified as Mound One. The mound reaches a height of approximately 30 feet and lies in mangroves. In 1566, a Spanish fort was established on the island, and Jesuits later sought to convert the Calusa to Catholicism; after three years, these futile efforts were wisely abandoned. In present times, all that remains is a trail with interpretive signs and some spectacular mounds for a flat South Florida. Exit US-75 on Corkscrew Road north of Naples. Proceed straight across US-41 for Koreshan State Historic Park. Turn north for a kayak outfitter located on the Estero River. From the outfitter to Mound Key is approximately 3.5 miles down the river and across the estuary. It is possible to join the Great Calusa Blueway, a paddling trail, from the Estero River for serious paddlers.

MOUNT ROYAL ARCHAEOLOGICAL SITE (Putnam County)

The area was inhabited by Native Americans from around 1200 A.D. to a little after 1500. Botanist and explorer John Bartram visited the site in 1765 and described the two mounds as Mount Royal in 1766. The mounds have been extensively excavated, beginning with Clarence Moore's efforts in 1894 and continuing in modern times in 1983, 1994, and 1995. The result has been over 38,000 artifacts, most of them Native American, some Spanish and British. Franciscans also had a mission in the area. The site is on The National Register of Historic Places. Information on the site is available from the Division of Historical Resources (see Appendix A). The site is located within Mount Royal Airport, which is just north of Lake George in Welaka off SR-309.

PHILIPPE PARK (Pinellas County)

Philippe Park's mounds are known as the Safety Harbor Site. The Safety Harbor Culture dates from the period between 1400 and 1700. The Smithsonian Institution conducted excavations led by Dr. Mathew W. Sterling in the 1930s. The mound excavated was purely ceremonial and located in the main village of the Tocobaga, a Timucuan-speaking tribe. The Tocobaga hunted small game and fished. The Tocobaga had a complex society, whose chief resided on the high Temple

WHO WAS ODET PHILIPPE?

The myths are many: nephew of King Louis XVI, Classmate of Napoleon, Surgeon General of Napoleon's Navy, captured by the British at the Battle of Trafalgar. Those are some of the legends that surround Odet Philippe, whose name has been misspelled over the years and is even misspelled on his tombstone.

Scholar, author, and direct descendant, J. Allison DeFoor, II, goes a long way toward setting the record straight. DeFoor reveals that Philippe was born too late to have been a classmate of Napoleon, much less Chief Surgeon in his Navy. However, it is known that Philippe practiced frontier doctoring and that might have accounted for the moniker Doctor Philippe. Historians can't even agree on Philippe's birth. It was thought that he was born in 1787 in Lyon France, but papers turned up in 1857 suggesting he might have been the child of a wealthy "Mulatto" in French Haiti. There is also questionable pirate lore concerning Philippe.

It is certain that Philippe established a plantation on the Pinellas Peninsula. He is thought to be the first orange grower to plant crops in rows. He married Marcia Booth and had a son, Odet "Keeter" Booth, who was the first white settler born on Peninsula Pinellas. The Gale of 1848 (a tremendous hurricane) did not harm Philippe's Helena Plantation, but allegedly Philippe put his son and wife atop the Indian mound to ride out the gale.

Mound with the village at the foot of the mound. The excavations revealed animal teeth, skulls, bones, shell and bone tools, projectile points, and pottery. A rare find was a bird effigy, now displayed at the Safety Harbor Museum of Regional History. From US-19 in Clearwater, go east on SR-60 (Gulf to Bay) and turn north on McMullen Booth Road before reaching Tampa Bay. Turn east on SR-580 and south on Bay Shore. Philippe Park is clearly announced by prominent signs and sits on Tampa Bay.

TIMUCUAN ECOLOGICAL AND HISTORIC PRESERVE (Duval County)

The Preserve is operated by the National Park Service and located along the north and south banks of the St. Johns River northeast of Jacksonville. Within the preserve, hikers may encounter shell mounds. The portion of the preserve on the south bank of the St. Johns is associated with Fort Caroline; it has reconstructed Timucuan huts as well as a reconstruction of Fort Caroline (the failed French outpost). The preserve land north across the St. Johns is the site of the Kingsley Plantation (treated separately under the African-American Heritage section of this book). From US-1 or I-95 south of Jacksonville, exit onto SR-9A north (from north of Jacksonville on I-95, take SR-9A south). Exit east on the south side of the St. Johns on Fort Caroline Road for the southern portion of the preserve; for the northern portion, cross the bridge and exit east on SR-105. There are prominent signs.

WEEDON ISLAND PRESERVE
(Pinellas County)

According to some reports, the area has been inhabited perhaps 7,000 years. It can now be explored by boardwalk, in the cultural center, atop an observation tower, and on a paddling trail through the mangroves. In 1972, the preserve was placed on the National Register of Historic Places. The Smithsonian Institution excavated the area beginning in 1923. The pottery and tools they dug up are used to describe a Weedon Culture. Every writer's nightmare! Archeologist Jesse Walter Fewkes called it "Weeden," and likewise historical works describe a "Weeden" Culture. The misspelling is still used. In addition to being a wonderful historical visit, the Preserve offers some exceptionally good birding. In St. Petersburg, US-92 (Gandy Boulevard) is an exit of I-275. Exit East on Gandy and proceed across 4th Street. The Preserve is to the south side of the road and prominently announced by signs.

WAKULLA SPRINGS ARCHEOLOGICAL AND HISTORIC DISTRICT (Wakulla County)

Wakulla Springs Archaeological and Historic District within Edward Ball Wakulla Springs State Park was designated as a historic and archaeological significant site in 1993. Remains of campsites, shell mounds, and animal-kill sites within the park's boundary suggest that Wakulla Springs has long been coveted for its abundant freshwater, game, and amazingly deep spring. In fact, the bottom of the spring bowl, some 180 feet deep, has yielded the bones of mastodons and ancient camels, and early Paleo-Indian relics. Now a state park and historic natural landmark, the 6,000-acre wildlife sanctuary features trails, swimming, and boat tours. From Tallahassee, go 16 miles south on SR-61/Wakulla Springs Road. Follow the signs and turn onto SR-267 at the flashing stoplight. Continue a few hundred feet to the park entrance on the right.

CONQUISTADORS

From the very beginning, Florida was beset with men who had grand plans for it, but these plans were often just as impractical as those of many who would follow in their footsteps in the centuries to come.

Juan Ponce de Leon died in 1521 probably believing that Florida was an island. His initial expedition to Florida in 1513 encountered many surprises, not the least of which was the Gulf Stream, which continually bedeviled navigators. There were also unfriendly Native Americans, who might have experienced earlier Spanish slaving expeditions. Modern legend has it that Ponce de Leon was in search of a so-called Fountain of Youth. His more important goals were gold and conquest. Ponce de Leon had served on the second voyage of Columbus in 1493 and led a brutal and successful invasion of Puerto Rico in 1506-7. His status as the ruler of that island changed when it was taken away from him and passed on to one of Columbus' sons in an unfair manner (unfair here is a relative term, giving how Puerto Rico was mercilessly taken away from its native inhabitants). The man, who named the state Florida (*La Florida*) for Easter flowers, was shot in the thigh during his second voyage with an arrow flung by a Calusa, probably in the San Carlos Bay area near Fort Myers. The arrow in his thigh did not kill him immediately; ensuing infection in a time of primitive medicine did what the Calusas could not.

In 1528, Pánfilo de Narváez led an ill-fated search for gold, which resulted in the death of 296 men, including him. Narváez, a redheaded giant with a patch over an eye lost in the Puerto Rican invasion (some say lost in Mexico with Cortez), in retrospect seems foolhardy and reckless to the point of having a death wish. The expedition landed near modern-day Tampa. Upon being told by perhaps clever locals that plentiful gold wasn't in their neck of the woods but found far to the north in the land of the Apalachee, Narváez's troops began a trek northward by land while promising to meet their transporting ships at a vaguely defined northern bay. It was a 250-mile (or so) march to the land of the Apalachee through wilderness. The Spaniards did not endear themselves to the Apalachee when they arrived. The first thing the invaders did was to seize the Apalachee chief and demand a gold ransom. Sixty-eight invaders were killed outright. The 242 survivors fled to the coast, likely around present-day St. Marks, where they found no waiting boats. The

boats were elsewhere—waiting and waiting in the wrong place. Narváez's desperate men built escape rafts tied together with the skin of their horses, which they killed and ate. On such questionable rafts, the soldiers set to sea, successfully departing Florida, only to encounter a probable hurricane in 1534. Four survivors walked into Mexico 14 years after they had set foot on *La Florida*. The rest had died. One survivor, Esteban, was an enslaved African.

Hernando de Soto arrived on the Gulf, probably at Tampa near Piney Point, in 1539. Piney Point is more or less where Port Manatee sits today. During his time in Florida, which occupied only a portion of his 3,700 mile trek over 10 states in search of gold, he enslaved natives, executed all the warriors of some groups, and had hands and noses chopped off captives in order to intimidate locals. Like his predecessors, he seized stores of grains and held hostage both chiefs and their daughters. In Florida, he forded at the very least the Alafia, Aucilla, Sante Fe, and Suwannee rivers (he named the Suwannee "Deer River"). On May 21, 1524, De Soto died of disease somewhere in what is present-day Arkansas. Before he died, many of his troops had succumbed to disease or enemy arrows. The most notable contributions of De Soto to the new world were: (1) pigs, which in the wild continue to plague Florida's wilderness as present-day feral hogs; and (2) diseases (measles, smallpox, and typhoid) that conquered Native Americans with no immunity much more effectively than De Soto ever did.

⋏ *An old photo of the entrance to St. Augustine.*

⋏ *The current replica of the old city gates.*

FLORIDA'S FRENCH CONNECTION: NOUVELLE FRANCE

It could be said of Jean Ribault, Huguenot leader, that if he had any luck in Florida, it was bad luck. In 1562, Protestant French forces headed for what they called "New France." Led by Jean Ribault, a settlement was built at Port Royal on the St. Johns, called "the May River" by the French for the month they arrived (hence a couple of decades later, the community of Mayport and Mayport Naval Station). When Ribault returned to Europe, he ended up delayed in returning, and thus failed to re-supply his outpost. His Port Royal was thus reduced to Native Americans and one Frenchmen, whom the Spanish would later take prisoner. A late effort was made to reinforce Port Royal when Rene de Laudonniere set sail on April 22, 1564. Finding Port Royal empty, Laudonniere established Fort Caroline located in the mouth of the St. Johns. However, the new settlement was not promptly re-supplied either, thus disheartened troops deserted, seized ships, and began to raid the Spanish in the Keys and Cuba, drawing attention to themselves and bringing Spanish retaliation. Ribaut for France and Pedro Menendez de Aviles for Spain arrived in Florida in 1565. Ribualt arrived at Fort Caroline intending to reinforce and defend it, only to be attacked shortly by the Spanish under Menendez. Ribault's ships retreated. Instead of Ribault, it was Menendez who established the first sustained settlement in North America, the city of St. Augustine. Ribault tried to attack the new settlement but was driven off. Menendez, who then sent soldiers to Fort Caroline, where he captured and executed all the French found there, while renaming the fort San Mateo. Ribault's fleeing ships wrecked, leading to his subsequent capture by Menendez. Along with his remaining men, Ribualt was put to death at what would be called Mantanzas, meaning a place of slaughter. This war atrocity has given its name to the river and fort called Matanzas for massacre.

You Say de Soto, I Say De Soto, Some Say Desoto

His proper name was Hernando de Soto. The word "soto" means grove in Spanish. Thus we have "Hernando of the grove" like we might have "Bill of the Bronx" or "Tarzan of the Apes." In modern times, his name has been given to a car, counties, streets, and monuments. It is DeSoto County in Florida, but Desoto County in Mississippi. If that is not puzzling enough, the name has appeared as De Soto, de Soto, Desoto, DeSoto, and deSoto.

ST. AUGUSTINE

The city of St. Augustine is named for the famous philosopher, theologian, and the author of many ancient classics, among them his *Confessions* and *The City of God*. A self-avowed sinner who converted late in life to the church at the urging of his mother and after a feeling of revelation, St. Augustine showed unusual mercy for his time in urging the sparing of heretics. Thus, there is some irony that the Spanish, who founded the city that was named for the great saint, instead of keeping French captives imprisoned, showed no mercy and slew them instead.

▲ *Spanish forces slaughtering the French Huguenots (Protestants).*

▲ *Jean Ribault and his troops.*

DE SOTO NATIONAL MONUMENT
(Manatee County)

In May 1539, Hernando de Soto landed along a bay in southwest Florida he named *"Espiritu Santo"* (probably Tampa Bay). Fresh from finding gold of the Incas under Pizarro, Hernando de Soto came armed with a commission from King Charles V to conquer and govern Florida. He arrived with 600-1000 men, 230 horses, a pack of war dogs, a cannon, muskets, armor, foodstuffs, and other supplies needed for this long journey. He was enthralled with native tales of "crystal, gold, rubies, and diamonds" that might be found here or perhaps northward in Florida's peninsula. The Memorial marks the beginning of the De Soto Trail somewhere "near here." The visitor center includes displays of Spanish armor, weapons, and other related items. A film orients the visitor about this chapter in history. On site are replicas of native Chickees (thatched huts), and the life of the Native Americans is captured by interpretive signage. Camp Uzita was built to resemble Hernando de Soto's base camp at the Indian Village of the same name. From I-75, exit west on SR-64 onto 75th Street West. It is 2.5 miles to the monument.

FORT CAROLINE NATIONAL MONUMENT (Duval County)

Historians are not quite certain where Fort Caroline was built or exactly where Ribault was killed. Fort Caroline National Monument contains a re-creation of Fort Caroline that in appearance, if not location, matches the best guesses historians are able to make. The national monument is operated by the National Park Service and includes an educational video. The monument is incorporated into Timucuan Ecological and Historical Preserve and includes hiking trails, a recreation of a Timucuan hut, and a monument to Ribaut. From I-95 or US-1 south of Jacksonville, exit onto SR-9A north. Exit east on Fort Caroline Road and follow the prominent signs.

⋏ *Festivities at De Soto National Monument with costumed performers.*

SPANISH COLONIZATION TO 1763

While Spain's first possession of Florida of more than 200 years was lengthy, it was always somewhat tenuous.

Initial Spanish expansion was led by adventurers in search of quick wealth and glory. Permanent settlements are about neither; rather they are about the grinding work of day-to-day living. The conditions within Florida for expansive settlement, however, were difficult.

St. Augustine, which was the most substantial Spanish settlement, was in essence a military outpost for most of its early existence. St. Augustine was attacked by the French, invaded by English pirates, and burned to the ground. Spanish rule of Florida from the city required the putting down on many rebellions among the Native American peoples. In 1597, the Guale, an Indian tribe in rebellion, brought in the French to assist them against Spain and the rebellion lasted until 1603. At various times, diseases like yellow fever ("yellow jack") and smallpox arrived in epidemic proportions to the detriment of the Native Americans.

Spain envisioned a Florida ruled by Spain with tribute paid by the Indians, who would all be converted to Catholicism. To this end, missions were established about Florida. The missions consisted of a few Spaniards, first Jesuits and later Franciscans, whose safety was in the hands of the chiefs of the people they hoped to convert. The missions to the Apalachee were supplied through the Fort of San Marcos de Apalachee, or St. Marks. Over 50 missions have been documented, and although none of them were successful over time, some lasted over 100 years. The "Mission Era" came to an abrupt end in 1704 during the War of Spanish Succession when the English from South Carolina, allied with Native Americans, destroyed the Apalachee missions, except those very near St. Augustine.

⋏ *Pedro Menendez de Avila sailed into St. Augustine harbor in 1565.*

MENENDEZ

From 1565 until his death in 1574, Pedro Menendez de Aviles was Adelantado, or Governor of Florida, appointed by the King of Spain, Phillip II. Menendez's achievements were defeating the French forces and establishing St. Augustine. Menendez wanted to create vast *estancias* or agricultural estates, which would be ruled over by the Spanish conquerors.

BATERIA DE SAN ANTONIO, GULF ISLANDS NATIONAL SEASHORE

(Escambia County)

The battery of St. Anthony still stands at Fort Barrancas within Gulf Islands National Seashore. Before the Spanish second rule over Florida, British forces had built a Royal Naval Redoubt (1763). The Spanish battery was built at the foot of the bluff in 1797 and a large portion still stands, unlike the naval redoubt. "Redoubt" is a word that has largely gone out of common usage, but means stronghold. It usually means there is a low wall from behind which soldiers do battle, a structure called a breastwork. Bateria de San Antonio and Fort Barrancas are physically located on-board Pensacola Naval Air Station, accessed from downtown Pensacola. Across the water on Santa Rosa Island lies Fort Pickens.

⋏ *Fort Barrancas*

⋏ *An aerial view of Castillo de San Marcos.*

⋏ *Castillo de San Marcos*

CASTILLO DE SAN MARCOS

(St. Johns County)

Translated, this is the Castle or Fort of St. Mark. Previous forts (there had been nine) were replaced at or near the current structure of coquina more than 300 years ago in 1695. Construction began 23 years earlier in 1672. Not only is St. Augustine the oldest and first U.S. city; it was another entranceway into the Matanzas River, an estuary through which boats could travel when St. Augustine was under siege. In 1702, during the War of the Spanish Succession, the English surrounded the fort for 50 days before they gave up and left. In 1740, once again a British siege led from Georgia was resisted, in large part because re-supplies could be brought up the Matanzas River. The importance of the Matanzas River mouth to the south was so important to the defense of St. Augustine that Fort Mantanzas was constructed beginning in 1740 and operational in 1742. Renamed Fort Marion once the U. S. acquired Florida in 1821, the fortress was used primarily as a prison for captured Native American such as Osceola, Coacoochee, and Geronimo. Castillo de San Marcos is a National Monument operated by the National Park Service. It is located on A1A in St. Augustine.

FLORIDA SPANISH COLONIAL HERITAGE TRAIL

Herencia Colonial Espania de Florida is a marvelous publication in both English and Spanish produced by the Division of Historical Resources. Included within its 68 pages are more than 100 sites and descriptions of how they relate to Florida's Spanish colonial rulers. See Appendix A for how to contact the Division of Historical Resources.

FORT MATANZAS NATIONAL MONUMENT
(St. Johns County)

The European history of the site begins with an incident 175 years before the construction of the fort at Matanzas – the Spanish massacre in 1565 of French forces on their way to attack St. Augustine, driven south by storms, and shipwrecked on the beach. The incident initiated Spanish control of Florida for 235 years and led to the naming of the Matanzas River (matanzas is Spanish for massacre).

Construction of the fort began in 1740 following the British siege of St. Augustine led by James Oglethorpe of Georgia. One reason St. Augustine survived this siege was that the Spanish were able to sneak in supplies from Cuba through the Matanzas Inlet. Consequently, this watchtower fort was built to guard this vulnerable "back door." Manned by only 6-10 men and armed with only five cannon, this little fort successfully held at bay at least two challenges by the British.

Today, the fort on Rattlesnake Island is reached by a passenger ferry that departs hourly from the visitor center dock. While waiting for the boat, visitors may view a short orientation film and/or walk a half-mile nature trail that is quite charming. Volunteer living history re-enactors are at the fort most Saturdays.

The entrance is on A1A, 14 miles south of St. Augustine at the southern tip of Anastasia Island.

GOVERNMENT HOUSE MUSEUM (St. Johns County)

The site on which the museum sits was in use during all colonial periods, spanning 1565 to 1821. Since then, it has housed a number of activities, including courthouse, customs house, post office, and now museum. A portion of it was also used as a hospital. The eastern wing was rebuilt in 1710 following its destruction by British forces in 1702. On display are a number of invaluable archaeological treasures. In St. Augustine, the museum is at 48 King Street. King Street is a street in the old city immediately south of the Bridge of the Lions.

MISSION OF NOMBRE DE DIOS (St. Johns County)

Tradition has it that Mendendez in 1565, upon landing and claiming St. Augustine for Spain, had the Catholic Church bless his efforts in a mass given by Father Francisco Lopez de Mendoza Grajeles, expedition chaplain. Today a cross rises 207 feet in commemoration. This cross was erected to celebrate the 400th anniversary of this event. "God's Mission" is in modern times home to The Shrine of Our Lady of La Leche. Rising from granite slabs, the cross weights 70 tons and consists of 200 panels of stainless steel. The site is located on A-lA in the northern portion of St. Augustine.

MISSION SAN LUIS DE TALIMALI (Leon County)

Centuries before Tallahassee housed politicians, college students, and public servants; the rolling hills around Florida's capitol sustained a large society of Native Americans that constructed ceremonial temple mounds. By 1633, as the Spanish mission system spread westward from St. Augustine, Franciscan friars arrived to Christianize the natives and build missions in Apalachee province. With a population of 1,400 natives, San Luis

⋏ *Fort Matanzas.*

de Talimali became the largest of Florida's missions. Between 1702 and 1704, however, the missions and their followers were all but obliterated by Governor James Moore and his Creek allies. As they attacked and destroyed the Spanish missions, many Apalachee were enslaved and several Franciscan friars killed. The devastation wrought by Moore's marauders effectively ended the mission system in Florida. 20th century excavations uncovered the foundations of the church and council house, which have been reconstructed. From I-10, take exit 28 to merge onto Capital Circle NW/SR-263 N. Turn right onto Tennessee Street (US-90) and follow it until signs appear on the left.

SAN MARCOS DE APALACHEE (Wakulla County)

Panfilo de Narvaez attempted to flee the Apalachee from St. Marks (a place that would become a strategic location at the confluence of the St. Marks and Wakulla Rivers) in 1528. When Hernando de Soto marched across the southeast, he was supplied from St. Marks by ships for a winter. Around 1650, a mission was built at St. Marks to convert the Apalachee. From this location the Spanish also supplied other missions in the region. During and after the British Period (1763-1783), Fort St Marks served as an important center for trade with the Creeks. St Marks was captured by U.S. forces during excursions against the Seminoles; little evidence remains of this near 350-year continuous occupation except for a plaque on the Tallahassee-St. Marks Trail, a bicycling and jogging path built on a former railroad bed.

The small town of St. Marks is located along US-98 to the west of Perry from US-19. Within it in recent years have been two excellent, laidback seafood restaurants and one bed and breakfast. Not far from the town is St. Marks National Wildlife Refuge, an exceptional place for hiking, wildlife observation, and a chance to see the St. Marks Lighthouse.

FROM THE HISTORICAL MARKER AT ST. MARKS:

Wooden stockades were built here by the Spanish in 1680 and 1758. In 1758, these were destroyed by a hurricane which drowned the garrison. A masonry fort was begun in 1759 but was soon abandoned to the Indians for a trading post and Indian rendezvous. It was occupied by the Spanish in 1783. General Andrew Jackson seized and occupied the fort in 1819. It became a U.S. possession in 1821 upon purchase of the territory from Spain. It was occupied as an army post until 1824 when the Indians were moved to a reservation. The Town of St. Marks was created by an act of Congress in 1830 and became a port of entry before railroads were extended to the seaboard. The fort was reestablished and occupied by the Confederate Army during the Civil War and the federal naval attack on the fort was repulsed in 1865.

British rule of Florida was brief—a mere 20 years. Britain gained Florida from the agreement ending the Seven Year's War (1756 to 1763), known in America as The French and Indian War. War's end saw Britain in possession of Havana, which the Spanish King Charles III found so intolerable he swapped Florida to get Cuba back. Britain in 1783 gave Florida back to Spain with the Treaty of Paris following the successful American Revolution.

British influence today is most noted by place names. Anxious to please their superiors, English surveyors named islands, rivers, and cities after their bosses, royalty, and the children of both. Thus the Earl of Hillsboro and his offspring have named in their honor a substantial amount of Florida.

One curious innovation: the British divided Florida into two units and ruled over East and West Florida. Western reaches, however, went as far as Lake Pontchartrain in present Louisiana; nonetheless, Florida as two separate entities (and even now as states) has often seemed to make sense. Politically and socially Northwestern and Southern Florida today are as different as day and night.

East and West Florida operated differently, the result of the personalities of their governors (James Grant, east, and George Johnstone, west, both Scots). Johnstone held a lottery to divvy up the land, not choosing land for himself until the 201st pick; while Grant lined up a prime plantation for himself almost immediately. Johnstone created the first legislature in 1766, five years before East Florida.

During the American Revolution (1776-1783), the British Floridas remained loyal to the Crown. East Florida became a refugee destination for Britain's beleaguered loyalist subjects escaping the southern colonies. Spain took advantage of the hostilities and battled England again. In 1779, the Spanish declared war on the British, and Bernardo De Galvez, Spanish Governor of Louisiana captured most of the English settlements on the Mississippi River and Gulf and Mexico, including Baton Rouge, Natchez, Mobile, and Pensacola. By the end of the war, the Spanish had recaptured West Florida. Despite the dream of dispossessed loyalists that East Florida would remain in British hands, the nation ceded both provinces back to Spain in the Paris Peace Conference (1783). Thus began the Second Spanish Period (1783-1821).

Spain's second tenure of 38 years was highlighted by Spanish decline, revolutionary upheavals in Spain and its new world colonies, and the aggressive encroachment by the new U.S. British presence and influence continued through trade, and contact with the Indians led to numerous border clashes with American settlers. In 1821, the Second Spanish Period came to an end after Andrew Jackson's invasion of Florida in the First Seminole War (1818). Jackson's temporary seizure of St. Marks and Pensacola eventually led to Spain's transfer of Florida to the U.S. under the Adams-Onis Treaty (1819) negotiated by Secretary of State John Quincy Adams. Spain formally transferred both Floridas to the U.S. in 1821.

THE CATHEDRAL PARISH (St. Johns County)

Also known as "the Cathedral," the Basilica of St. Augustine is the nation's oldest Catholic parish. Although the church has been rebuilt several times over the centuries, the parish community has remained intact since the first Mass in 1565 was held to celebrate the founding of St. Augustine. Located near the Bridge of Lions at 38 Cathedral Place, the current church was constructed after an 1887 fire and retains portions of the original walls and façade. In the 1970s, following further renovations, the church was designated as a National Historic Landmark and elevated by Pope Paul VI to a Minor Basilica. From I-95, take Exit #318. Turn east on SR-16 to US-1. Turn left at CR-214/West King Street. Turn left at Charlotte Street, then left at Cathedral Place.

COLONIAL SPANISH QUARTER MUSEUM (St. Johns County)

Located on 1.5 acres in the heart of the city, St. Augustine's Colonial Spanish Quarter showcases the lives of Spanish soldiers, tradesmen, and their families during the 1740s. The open-air, living-history museum depicts the area's past through reconstructed dwellings and artifacts found locally and from Florida shipwrecks. Amid the sounds and smells of carpentry and candle making, visitors passing through the narrow streets of the pedestrian-only complex stroll among costumed-clad interpreters eager to share the occupations, customs, and folkways of 18th century Florida. The Colonial Spanish Quarter Museum is located at 29 St. George Street. This location is in a pedestrian-only portion of the city of St. Augustine. It is probably best to park at the Historic Downtown Parking Facility on West Castillo Drive and proceed to St. George Street on foot. From I-95, SR-207 leads to St. Augustine. Once downtown, it is next to impossible to miss Castillo de San Marcos and Castillo Drive.

FORT SAN CARLOS DE BARRANCAS (Nassau County)

The Spanish built the fort in 1816 only to have it fall to Scottish adventurer, Gregor MacGregor in 1817, a general in the service of the Latin American revolutionary republics of New Granada and Venezuela. It was here that MacGregor raised his famous "Green Cross of Florida" flag. MacGregor's scheme to use Amelia Island to attack Spanish East Florida was shortlived. He was succeeded in turn by his some-time collaboraor, the pirate Luis Aury. American authorities, determined to shut down illegal slave trading and other actitivies interceded in 1817. The site on a bluff on the northern westerm tip of Amelia Island overlooking the Amelia River has a majetic view of this stratgic waterway into the interior. The historic marker is located on Fernandina Beach. From I-95 approaching the Georgia border, Fernandina is accessed by taking A1A to the east.

THE GONZALEZ-ALVAREZ HOUSE/THE OLDEST HOUSE (St. Johns County)

The Gonzalez-Alvarez House, often refered to as The Oldest House, is the oldest documented colonial Spanish house in Florida. The site, three blocks south of the Plaza de la Constitucion, has been continually occupied since the early 1600s. The original wood-thatched, one-story dwelling was destroyed during early 18th century raids on the city and rebuilt using coquina stone (limestone composed of shell fragments). The historical landmark encompasses Spanish, British, and American architectural elements. Named for two of its most prominent owners, St. Augustine's quaint Gonzalez-Alvarez House is part of the Oldest House Museum Complex located at 14 Saint Francis Street. From I-95, take Exit 318. Turn east on SR-16 to US-1. Turn left at CR-214/West King Street. Turn right at St George, then left at Saint Francis Street.

OLDEST HOUSE MUSEUM COMPLEX/TOVAR HOUSE (St. Johns County)

Next door to the Gonzalez–Alvarez House, in the Oldest House Museum Complex, sits the Tovar House. It is named for a Spanish soldier, Jose Tovar, who occupied the house during the final days of Spain's first Spanish period that came to an end in 1763. Following the return of Florida to the Spanish two decades later, Geronimo Alvarez purchased the property, which remained in his family until 1871. From I-95 southbound, exit at SR–16 and turn left. Go to US–1 and turn right. Turn left on King Street, then right on Avenida Menendez. The road bends 90 degrees and becomes St. Francis Street. The house will be on the right.

PENSACOLA HISTORIC DISTRICT/SEVILLE SQUARE
(Pensacola and Escambia counties)

The earliest known attempts at European settlement were not the so-called "lost colonies" or the arrival of Pilgrims in New England; rather, the first Spanish attempts to permanently dwell in the U.S. occurred here beginning in 1559. The district itself holds some remains from those times, and hurricane survivors built structures within the historic district. When Spain recaptured Pensacola from the British in 1781, the street names were changed to Spanish and remain so to this day. Within the historic district is the T. T. Wentworth, Jr., Florida State Museum, which contains artifacts from a shipwreck in 1559, including the anchor believed to be that of Don Tristan De Luna's, the Spanish sailor who founded Pensacola. Also inside the district are St. Michaels Cemetery and Old Christ Church, the oldest cemetery and church in Florida. A number of highways lead into Pensacola from I-10 and proceed to the heart of the city.

WASHINGTON OAKS GARDENS STATE PARK (St. Johns County)

The Park is nestled between the Matanzas River and the Atlantic Ocean on the Intercoastal Waterway. The picturesque landscape has had several prominent owners from Lieutenant Governor John Moultrie to General Joseph Hernandez, who was responsible for capturing Osceola during the Second Seminole War (1835-1842). The land, called Bella Vista, was eventually sold to a distant relative of President George Washington, leading to the moniker of Washington Oaks. Louise Powis Clark, a New York designer, purchased the property in 1936, and it became the winter home for her and her third husband Owen D. Young. They are responsible for the development of the property. The visitor center was once their home. The log cabin gift shop was Mr. Young's office. The gardens were transferred to the State of Florida in 1960. Featuring towering moss–draped oaks, nature trails, and tranquil gardens, the 425-acre park is located at 6400 North Oceanshore Blvd, 2 miles south of Marineland off A1A.

⋀ *Washington Oaks Gardens State Park.*

⋀ *The rocky shoreline at Washington Oaks Gardens State Park.*

AFRICAN-AMERICAN HERITAGE

The history of African Americans in Florida extends backwards in time to the European encounter. Blacks (both slave and free) were among the Spanish explorers and first settlers of Florida. Both Spanish and British colonists brought slaves to America.

By 1700, perhaps 500,000 African Americans had been enslaved and sent to what would become the U.S. By the 1800s, the number of slaves within the U.S. exceeded 10 million. A relatively small population of free blacks lived in the U.S. as well.

Before 1821 when Florida became an American territory, many African Americans lived in isolated "maroon" settlements in the southern peninsula and near Seminole Indian towns. Not long after the establishment of the territory, sizeable slave plantations were established in "Middle Florida," the region near present-day Tallahassee. In that area, a social and economic society that mirrored what had been established in other regions of the "Old South" flourished. Even though slaves were largely concentrated in north Florida counties, African Americans accounted for 43% of Floridians on the eve of the Civil War. In the central and southern peninsula things were different; there the frontier prevailed. Seminoles and their black allies farmed, hunted, and herded cattle in relative seclusion until white pioneers (sometimes known as Crackers) moved into these lands. By the 1830s, friction among the whites and the Seminoles and blacks, including attempts to force the latter back into slavery, led to the Second Seminole War (1836-1842).

During the Civil War, African Americans may have accompanied their masters to battlefields outside Florida, but the vast majority toiled on farms, or were sometimes conscripted into wartime duties such as salt making and fort building. Some took the opportunity to escape slavery and joined invading Union armies. (This was especially true of slaves known as the "contrabands" who lived along the St. Johns River.) Large numbers of blacks served in Florida as part of the famed 54th Massachusetts, a history of which is depicted in the stirring movie "Glory."

After the Civil War, blacks, on their own initiative, and assisted by such institutions as the Freedman's Bureau, the American Missionary Association, and religiously affiliated organizations, sought education and land with enthusiasm. The Fourteenth and Fifteenth Amendment to the U.S. Constitution afforded legal equality and voting rights. During Reconstruction (1865-1877), blacks voted, held office, and participated in politics largely within the Republican Party. While Reconstruction opened many political, economic, and social opportunities, many of its efforts at establishing equality and full political rights were flawed and eventually were thwarted when white Democratic rule resumed in 1877. Gilded Age and Progressive Era Florida (1877-1920) represented a "nadir" for Blacks as segregation became institutionalized through state law and the Supreme Court case *Plessey vs. Ferguson* (1896) that affirmed the policy of "separate but equal." Florida also led the nation in lynching per capita.

In 2008, the legislature of Florida passed a resolution apologizing for its role in slavery. The resolution cited some of the more cruel punishments meted out to slaves such as nailing a slave's ears to a post and lashing a slave with a whip. Such punishments indicate a degree of brutality few of us in modern-day America can imagine. Unfortunately, brutal treatment and mob lynching continued into the twentieth century. James Baldwin's immortal short-story, "Going to Meet the Man," recreates the horror of a lynching in many ways similar to some that occurred in Florida.

If the story of African Americans in Florida is one of suffering, it is also one of victory of the spirit. If it is a story of hate and despair, it also is the story of love and hope. The history of African Americans has in recent years finally received its due. Largely gleaned from oral story-telling traditions and old documents, the significant contribution of black Americans to Florida is beginning to be fully recognized.

Education has always figured prominently in the efforts of African Americans to receive equal treatment. Florida has had four historically black universities that have traditionally been composed of African Americans and still are primarily African American in student body and faculty. These include: Bethune-Cookman, Florida A&M University, Florida Memorial College, and Edward Waters College. Three of the four were started during Reconstruction; Bethune-Cookman was founded in 1904.

Segregation of the races essentially followed Reconstruction and often became codified in law as well as tradition. Segregation never meant fair treatment of the races, but separate and inferior treatment for those of African-American descent. The result of segregation was often the formation of flourishing African-American communities within large Florida cities such as Jacksonville, Tampa, Orlando, Miami, and Bartow. Florida also had one of the first all black communities in Eatonville, near Orlando. The Civil Rights Movement of the 1950s and 60s swept through Florida as well as the nation. The Tallahassee Bus Boycott (1956) and the racial conflict in St. Augustine (1964) are but two Florida events with significant national connotations.

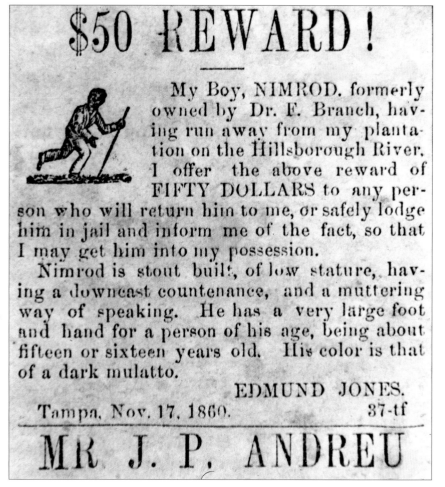

▲ *An 1860 advertisement in Tampa offering a reward for the return of a runaway slave.*

AMERICAN BEACH (Nassau County)

The spirit of American Beach continues to exist in memory—and in a small park beside the timeless Atlantic Ocean and its shifting sands. As incredible as it seems now, African Americans were largely excluded from the Gulf of Mexico and the Atlantic Ocean only five decades ago; in fact, during the Civil Rights movements, attempts by integrated groups to pray on beaches as far apart as Clearwater and Jacksonville were met by arrests and mobs. The Pension Bureau of the Afro-American Life Insurance Company, led by A. L. Lewis, developed American Beach as a resort for black Americans. Land purchase and development began in 1935 and was completed in 1946. The area had been home to freedmen since at least 1862, when Union forces established the free community of Franklintown. Famous African Americans who were guests at American Beach included the late James Brown and Ray Charles, and such earlier entertainers as Cab Calloway and Ossie Davis. American Beach is on the east side of A1A south of Fernandina at the southern end of Amelia Island.

⋏ *Abandoned building at American Beach.*

BETHUNE-COOKMAN COLLEGE
(Volusia County)

A child of slaves, Mary McLeod Bethune founded a school for girls in 1904 with operating funds of $1.50. At that time her school was intended for African-American girls. One of the many negative effects of slavery and "Jim Crow" was the denial of education to African Americans. Mary Bethune's school for girls grew into a high school in 1923 when it merged with the Cookman Institute of Jacksonville, a school for African-American boys. In 1941, Bethune-Cookman College began state-approved four-year programs in the liberal arts and education. In the 1970s, the programs were expanded with an enrollment exceeding 2,000 in modern times. Mary McLeod Bethune worked closely with Eleanor Roosevelt and was a consultant of her husband, serving in his "Black Cabinet," an informal advisory group that advised the president on issues related to African Americans. She attended the founding meeting of the United Nations and served as Director of Black Affairs in the National Youth Administration, during the New Deal. The college campus is located in Daytona Beach, exiting from I-95.

➤ *Mary McLeod Bethune, 1915.*

L. B. BROWN HOUSE (Polk County)

Born to a plantation minister nearly a decade before the ending of slavery, Lawrence Bernard Brown overcame the adversities and demoralizing effects of slavery to become a successful entrepreneur and East Bartow civic leader. Brown, a self-taught carpenter, constructed and sold dozens of houses to the area's swelling black population during the late 19th and early 20th centuries. Built for his family of 11 children, The L. B. Brown House is one of the last remaining structures in Florida to be constructed and owned by a former slave. The opulent 1,700 square-foot Victorian home at 470 2nd Avenue is a nationally registered historic landmark and museum. From I-4 east of Tampa, take Exit 48 for CR-557 South toward Winter Haven/Lake Alfred. Merge onto CR-557/Old Grade Road and follow CR-557/South Buena Vista Drive for approximately 6 miles. Turn right at US-17-92 and immediately merge left at US-17 South. Continue on US-17 for 15 miles. Turn right at East Main Street, and then turn left at South 2nd Avenue.

EATONVILLE (Orange County)

The African-American town of Eatonville was founded on Christmas Eve 1886. It is the oldest surviving town of more than 100 black townships established before 1900. Among its famous citizens were the writer Zora Neale Hurston and the football player, David "Deacon" Jones, a truly big man, who was best known as a star of the Baltimore Colts. Eatonville is north of Orlando off I-4 and near Winter Park to the east and south of Maitland. A ZORA! Festival is held each January, where the Zora Neale Hurston National Museum of Fine Arts is located.

FLORIDA AGRICULTURAL AND MECHANICAL UNIVERSITY

(Leon County)

Florida A&M University, one of Florida's 11 state universities, was created in 1887, as the State Normal College for Colored Students. It began with an enrollment of 15 students with two instructors. The Tallahassee institution has grown steadily over its more than 12 decades into a 419-acre campus with over ten thousand students, and has become a leader in annual recruitment of National Achievement Scholars. Re-named as a university in 1953, and lovingly nicknamed FAMU (*pham u*), it is on the National Register of Historic Places. A former Carnegie library, now the Black Archives, displays artifacts of the African-American experience. Its colleges now include a law

school (in Orlando), a pharmacy school, and a nursing school. From I-10 in Tallahassee, take exit 209A and merge onto Mahan Drive/SR-10 /US-90 toward Tallahassee. Turn left at North Meridian Street. Turn right at East Park Avenue. Turn left at South Monroe Street. Turn right at Oakland Avenue East/FAMU Way, then left at South Martin Luther King Jr. Blvd.

FORT GADSDEN/APALACHICOLA NATIONAL FOREST (Franklin County)

The site contains the remains of two forts located on the Apalachicola River. The first fort served as a post for British troops and their allies of ex-slaves and local Native Americans during the War of 1812. The British evacuated Florida in 1815, leaving arms, cannon, and gunpowder for several hundred African Americans and a few dozen Seminoles and Creeks that remained. Word of the "Negro Fort" attracted hundreds of runaways, enflaming Southern slave owners. After several border incidents, U.S. military forces were ordered to attack. A hot shot fired by an American gunboat ignited the fort's powder magazine, destroying the structure, and killing most of the inhabitants. Under the supervision of U. S. Army Lt. James Gadsden, a new fort was constructed nearby. The ruins are a silent witness of those willing to die for freedom rather than live in servitude. The site is off of SR-65 (an exit off I-10 that connects with US-98). The fort is 6 miles south of Sumatra.

FORT MOSE HISTORIC STATE PARK

(St. Johns County)

More than 100 escaped English slaves from the colony of South Carolina lived in the village of Garcia Real de Santa Teresa de Mose (Fort Mose) in Spanish Florida north of Castillo de San Marcos in St. Augustine. The Africans were organized into a slave militia in 1726 and in 1738 built the first Fort Mose, where they lived with their families. The town was relocated in 1752 and abandoned in 1763, when Florida became a British colony. Both sites of Fort Mose have become absorbed into marshland about 2 miles north of St. Augustine. A state park has been created at the approximate site. It is just north of St. Augustine on the east side of US-1.

HIGGS BEACH CEMETERY

(Monroe County)

Key West's Higgs Beach was the final resting-place for nearly 300 Africans found aboard ships intercepted by the U.S. Navy. Although the slave trade into the country had been outlawed in the U.S. since 1808,

slavers continued peddling human cargo in Cuba and Brazil. In 1860, U.S. Navy blockades stopped three American-owned slave ships transporting some 1,400 enslaved Africans. Those who had perished during the voyage from harsh conditions were buried at Higgs Beach, and the survivors sent to Liberia. Civil War fortifications were built over the burial grounds, and the entombed seemed to be forever forgotten. However, nine of the graves were rediscovered, and in 2001 a state historical marker was placed at the site between White Street Pier and West Martello Tower. From US-1 in Key West, turn right at N Roosevelt Boulevard, and turn left at White Street. Higgs Beach is located along Atlantic Boulevard between White and Reynolds Streets.

JUAN GARRIDO

When Ponce de Leon voyaged to Florida in 1513, with him was a free African named Juan Garrido. Garrido was a conquistador participating of his own free will, who had fought in the Spanish subjugation of Hispaniola (now Haiti and the Dominican Republic) and Puerto Rico. Slaves and freemen were present almost from the conception of St. Augustine, America's oldest inhabited city.

WHAT WAS 'JIM CROW'

The term Jim Crow was used to describe segregationist behaviors enforced through both custom and law. The origin of the term is debated. But a crow is black, and Jim is an easy, short name. Jim Crow laws and customs were strongest in the South, but felt elsewhere in the nation.

⋏ *A building reconstructed of tabby at the Kingsley Plantation.*

THE KINGSLEY PLANTATION (Duval County)

Operated by the National Park Service, the Kingsley Plantation is a premier experience on Florida's Black Heritage Trail. Florida's plantation period lasted from roughly 1763 to the end of the Civil War in 1865. Zephaniah Kingsley was a white plantation owner from 1814 to 1837. Anta Madgigine Jai, from Senegal, was a slave Kingsley purchased in 1806 while in Havana, Cuba. Kingsley took Anta for his wife and business partner, and they had two sons and two daughters. When Florida became a U.S. territory, the relatively tolerant Spanish attitude toward interracial marriages vanished. Spanish tolerance was replaced by harsh American laws restricting the rights of "persons of color" to intermarry or own property. If Kingsley died under the laws then in existence, his family would have lost their freedom. In 1837, Kingsley moved his family to the free Republic of Haiti. The house is well restored and preserved. On the grounds are the remnants of buildings and slave quarters built from a material known as "tabby," a concoction of oyster shell, lime, sand, and water. From I-95 north of Jacksonville, exit east on SR-105/A1A. The turn to the site is a plainly marked. The Kingsley Plantation is on the northern tip of Fort George Island at the Fort George Inlet off A1A.

MOUNT ZION BAPTIST CHURCH
(Dade County)

Mt. Zion Church, a two-story Mediterranean revival-style structure near the county courthouse, is home to one of Miami's oldest African-American congregations. It replaced a simple late 19th century palm-thatched wood structure destroyed by a 1926 hurricane. Construction of the large concrete-and-stucco house of worship began on the eve of the Great Depression and was completed just prior to America's entrance into WWII. Located at 301 NW 9th Street in the predominately African American community of Overton, access is private and restricted. Mt. Zion Baptist church was listed in the National Register of Historical Places in the late 1980s. From I-95 S in Miami, exit at NW 8th Street. Turn left at NW 8th Street. Turn left at NW 3rd Avenue, then left at NW 9th Street.

ROSEWOOD (Levy County)

The town of Rosewood lies along SR-24 between US-19 and Cedar Key. What transpired in Rosewood at the beginning of January 1923 is the stuff of nightmares. Today, only a plaque exists to remind Floridians of the horrible events. People died in Rosewood in a violent racial clash. Six of the known dead were African Americans and two were white. The spark was an alleged assault on a white woman (Fanny Taylor) by a black man (Jesse Hunter), an allegation that is believed by historians to be false; the black community instead believed that Fanny Taylor had sexual relations with a boyfriend and fabricated the tale for the benefit of her husband. When the black community attempted to resist attacking white mobs, the conflagration consumed every black-owned building in Rosewood, including churches, and resulted in the vanquishing of African Americans from their homes and their land. Compensation was provided through legislation to survivors many years after the tragic events. Rosewood and myriad persecutions during this era reflect a sad period when economic power came from mob violence, and segregation was enforced through even more violent intimidation.

⋎ *The smoldering ruins of homes destroyed by the violence at Rosewood.*

TERRITORY AND STATEHOOD

Three years before Florida became a U.S. Territory, General Andrew Jackson led campaigns into Spanish Florida with the intent of driving Spain out. Jackson's mission was to chastise Indians bands near the international boundary and kill or capture British soldiers and traders who were assisting them. In the First Seminole War (1818) Jackson burned several Indian villages, captured two British subjects (a soldier and a trader) and executed them at St. Marks. Jackson's unauthorized action was controversial at the time and led to a Congressional investigation that eventually cleared him of wrongdoing. Spain protested the action but ceded Florida to the U.S. in 1819 in the Adams-Onis Treaty.

Andrew Jackson was the territory's first governor, but soon after he presided over the transfer of flags, he resigned, and was succeeded by William P. DuVal, for whom Duval County is named (indeed, Florida has a Jackson County also and a Jacksonville).

Despite attempts by Georgia and Alabama to acquire parts of Florida and efforts from interests in the eastern part of the territory to make Florida two territories, it remained one administrative unit.

Florida's first Legislative Council met in Pensacola. DuVal called for the session on June 10, but it could not begin until July 22 because several delegates from the east were shipwrecked along the way, thus delayed. When they arrived, the assembly was threatened with yellow fever and moved north. Before their deliberations were over, two of the council members were dead. Subsequently, DuVal appointed John Lee Williams and Dr. William H. Simmons to find another spot for meetings; they picked the site of the future capitol of Tallahassee, a midway point between Pensacola and St. Augustine.

Despite mixed views among Floridians over becoming part of the Union, the territory moved toward statehood, holding a constitutional convention in St. Joseph (modern-day Port St. Joe). A proposed constitution was approved on January 11, 1839. In May, the voters passed it, but Florida has to wait another six years until it could join the Union as the 27th state. On March 3, 1845 Florida joined the Union as a slave state, thus balancing the admission of free-state Iowa.

The early policies of the territory were quite clear: move, kill, or expel the Seminoles from desirable lands, and eventually all of Florida, and bring in white settlement, which would promote industry. These policies were not unlike those of the western territories.

The Treaty of Moultrie Creek (1823): Seminoles were removed from northern Florida to a reservation between the Peace and Withlacoochee rivers. Then, efforts were begun to force the Seminoles west. After the Indian Removal Act (1832), federal authorities negotiated the Treaty of Payne's Landing by which the Seminoles agreed to inspect lands in the Arkansas Territory for the purpose of relocating. Subsequent disputes led to the Second Seminole War (1836-1842). By the mid 1880s, it is reported that less than 200 Seminoles remained in Florida out of thousands – and those remaining were in hiding and feared for their lives and freedom.

By the 1850s, Florida and other Southern states became increasingly disenchanted with the Union. After Abraham Lincoln was elected President in 1860 on a platform to exclude slavery from the territories, Florida joined other Southern states in its decision to secede from the Union. On January 3, 1861, Florida became the third state to leave; and this less than 15 years after it had joined the Union.

AUDUBON HOUSE AND TROPICAL GARDENS (Monroe County)

Visiting here is a stroll through mid-19th century Key West history and customs. Built by Captain John H. Geiger, the house is a majestic example of American classic-revival architecture. John James Audubon, who visited the area in 1832, painted and catalogued Florida birds for his Birds of America series. Many of the birds were seen on Geiger's property. The one-acre site offers self-guided tours throughout the house and exotic landscape. From US-1 South in Key West, turn right at North Roosevelt Boulevard. Turn right at Whitehead Street.

CHESTNUT STREET CEMETERY
(Franklin County)

Tucked between Apalachicola's 6th and 8th Streets on US-98, Chestnut Street Cemetery is one of the oldest and most significant graveyards on Florida's Gulf Coast. It was established in 1831, while Florida was still a U.S. territory. Also known as The Old City Graveyard, the site's fading and crumbling headstones reflect its age, but many dates and epitaphs are still legible. Interred in the cemetery are the remains of Apalachicola's founders and defenders of the 19th century seaport. From sailors and early civic leaders, to soldiers of the Confederacy and victims of yellow fever, this graveyard chronicles the area's colorful history.

CONSTITUTIONAL CONVENTION STATE MUSEUM (Gulf County)

The museum is located just to the north of US-98 in the town of Port St. Joe, Florida. The early Constitution approved there before statehood is not the one currently in use. In fact, Florida's defining document has been redrawn many times. The museum has excellent displays and a re-creation of the room where the 1838 State Constitutional Convention was held.

DIAL-GOZA HOUSE (Madison County)

The Dial-Goza house, built approximately in 1880, was placed on the National Register of Historic Places in 1973. The house is named for a Confederate Major, William H. Dial. Dial's house was built in Italian style, including a cupola on the roof and millwork. The Dial-Goza house is located at Range and Marian Streets in the town of Madison along I-10 and to the east of Tallahassee.

DOW MUSEUM OF HISTORIC HOUSES
(St. Johns County)

Dow Museum is a collection of historical homes and peaceful gardens built between 1790 and 1910. Eight preserved buildings display furnishings and collections from St. Augustine's extensive history dating from colonial times to the early 20th century. Among the houses was the one built in the 1790 visited by Prince Achille Murat of France. Dow Museum is located south of the Casa Monica Hotel on Cordova Street. The Village offers time traveling of the imagination in America's oldest city. From I-95, take Exit #318. Turn east on SR-16 to US-1 South/N. Ponce de Leon Blvd. Turn left at CR-214/King Street. Turn right at Cordova.

GOVERNOR'S MANSION (Leon County)

In the 20th and 21st centuries, Florida's governors have lived in three different governor's mansions while governing the state. The first Governor's Mansion was built on this site in 1907. It lasted through 15 governors (Broward, Gilchrist, Trammell, Catts, Hardee, Martin, Carlton, Sholtz, Cone, Holland, Caldwell, Warren, McCarty, Johns, and Collins) until 1955, when it was torn down and the present structure erected. The "Grove" (see below) temporarily functioned as the Governor's Mansion from 1955-56. The present mansion, completed in 1956, was designed by Palm Beach architect Marion Syms Wyeth. In addition to reception and dining rooms, portions open for public tour (and virtual tour) include The Manatee Garden. Special and group tours are available by appointment. Regularly scheduled tours vary. It is best to check in advance (see the information in Appendix A). The mansion is located at 700 North Adams Street in downtown Tallahassee.

THE GROVE (Call/Collins House) (Leon County)

Florida's third and fifth territorial governor, Richard Keith Call, constructed The Grove in the 1830s. Also known as the Call/Collins House, the structure became the permanent residence of Mary Call Darby Collins, the great-granddaughter of Governor Call and wife of Governor LeRoy Collins. The privacy of Mrs. Collins was paramount during her residency. Mrs. Collins passed away toward the end of 2009 and since then, efforts are underway to renovate the building.

KEY WEST CEMETERY (Monroe County)

The Key West Cemetery is as unique as the subtropical island city itself. Along the winding paths and fading tombs of this 19-acre, mid-19th century graveyard, unusual statues and sculptures are set among quirky epitaphs such as B. P. Roberts tongue-in-cheek inscription: "I Told You I Was Sick." Relocated to Solace Hill a year after an 1846 hurricane destroyed a smaller beachfront location, the cemetery houses over 70,000 graves. Although no new souls are placed to rest here, the site is open daily for sightseers and guided tours are available. From US-1 South into Key West: turn (right at North Roosevelt Boulevard. Turn right at Windsor Lane, then right at Passover Lane. The main entry gates are at the intersection of Passover Lane, Margaret and Angela Streets.

OLD CITY CEMETARY (Leon County)

According to differing sources, "Tallahassee" in the language of the Apalachee meant either "old town" or "old fields." The Old City Cemetery contains the bones of those who came after the Apalachee. Buried there are Civil War bluecoats, confederates, settlers, slaves, and a French prince (Murat) and his wife. The Cemetary is located between Call Street and Park Avenue in the City of Tallahassee, which lies along I-10.

PENA-PECK HOUSE (St. Johns County)

Named for two of its most prominent residents, the house was constructed in the mid-18th century for the Spanish Royal Treasurer, Juan de Pena. Following Florida's first Spanish period, British diplomats resided in the two-story, wood-and-coquina home situated on the corner of Treasury and St. George streets. Dr. Seth Peck later purchased the property, which remained in his family's care for nearly a century before being gifted to the city as a house museum in 1931. The St. Augustine Women's Exchange, the area's oldest civic organization, has restored and currently maintains this historic home. From I-95 take Exit #318. Turn east on SR-16 to U.S-1 South/North Ponce de Leon Blvd. Turn left at Orange Street. Turn right at Cordova Street then left on Treasury Street.

SEGUI-KIRBY SMITH HOUSE (St. Johns County)

One of three dozen surviving Spanish Colonial homes in St. Augustine, the Segui-Kirby Smith House dates from the late 18th century. The site, on the corner of Artillery Lane and Avilles Street at 6 Artillery Lane, has continuously been occupied since the 1500s. In 1786, Bernardo Segui, a successful merchant and Spanish military official, resided in the house. It was also the birthplace of Confederate General Edmund Kirby Smith in 1824. Donated as a public library in 1895, the three-story structure currently serves as a historical research library for the St. Augustine Historical Society and is open to the public. From I-95, take Exit #318. Turn east on SR-16 to US- 1 South. Turn left at CR-214/King Street. Turn right at St George, then left at Artillery Lane.

STATE CAPITOL (Leon County)

William P. DuVal, who became the first civilian governor, oversaw the founding of the territorial capitol of Tallahassee in 1824. A wing of the permanent capitol was built in 1826 but was later torn down. Another building was completed in 1845. The Old Capital now houses a Florida political history museum with extensive exhibits. The Capitol Complex consists of the Old Capitol, the New Capitol, and the House and Senate Office Buildings. My, how things have grown: the modern capitol is 22 stories, has 14 elevators, and is the workplace for 3,000 human beings when the legislature is not in session (and perhaps 4,500 when it is). The capitol is open for public tours, but it is best to check the schedule before a visit (see Appendix A). The capitol is in downtown Tallahassee and prominently announced by signs.

TRINITY EPISCOPAL PARISH (St. Johns County)

St. Augustine's Trinity Episcopal Parish at the intersection of St. George and King streets is Florida's oldest Protestant church. The church's first services began in 1821 in a small 1,800 square-foot coquina structure. Following decades of additions and repairs, the neo-gothic structure now holds over 500 parishioners. The church features some of the oldest stained-glass windows found throughout the Episcopal Diocese of Florida, with one constructed by the prestigious glass artist Louis Comfort Tiffany. The historic parish recently purchased a neighboring 6,000 square-foot building (Trinity Hall) to serve its growing 21st century congregation and the local community. From I-95, take Exit #318. Turn east on SR-16 to US-1 South/N. Ponce de Leon Blvd. Turn left at CR-214/W King Street. Turn right at St George.

UNION BANK BUILDING (Leon County)

Built in 1830 for William Williams, Tallahassee's Union Bank was the city's first bank and is Florida's oldest remaining financial building. The Union Bank was chartered in 1833 and opened its doors in January 1835, with John G. Gamble as president. It was capitalized at $1,000,000 and became territorial Florida's principal financial institution, until the Panic of 1837, Indian Wars, and unsound practices closed its doors in 1843. Under various names and ownership, Union Bank played a vital role in the community by serving cotton planters, and after the Civil War it housed the Freedman's Bank, assisting the economic affairs of emancipated slaves. Since then, a wide variety of businesses operated from the structure prior to its 1971 relocation from Adams Street to 219 Apalachee Parkway. Now serving as an extension of Florida A&M University's Black Archives, the building houses a museum and research center that displays many African American artifacts and is open to the public by reservation, From I-10 in Tallahassee, take Exit 209A and merge onto Mahan Dr/SR-10/US-90 heading toward Tallahassee. Turn left at North Calhoun Street/CR-1559 S. Turn left at Apalachee Pkwy/SR-20/US-2.

DAVID LEVY YULEE

▲ *Senator David Yulee, 1850.*

He came from wealth. His father, Moses Elias Levy, a Sephardic Jew, came to Florida in 1818 in possession of title for 60,000 acres purchased from a Spanish merchant. Originally, like his namesake, Moses, the elder Levy had a vision of a promised land filled with Jewish settlers, but these Jews were not fleeing from Egypt but from Europe. When resettlement efforts failed, he purchased slaves to run what became his plantations.

After a falling out with his father, David Levy added the ancestral "Yulee" to his name. He read law in St. Augustine, entered politics, and was elected as Florida's territorial delegate to Congress in 1841, serving until Florida became a state. Ironically, when territorial delegate, Levy lobbied for statehood, and when Florida was a state, he became one of the first two U.S. Senators; yet he was also a fervent, "fire-breathing" Southern politician and called for secession. He also became a Confederate Congressman.

Levy's efforts were instrumental in developing Florida's transportation facilities. He built the first cross-state railroad that ran from Fernandina to Cedar Key that opened just as the Civil War began. The West Coast city of Yulee and the county named Levy are in his honor. Yulee also holds the distinction of being the first practicing Jew to become a member of the U.S. Senate. See Yulee Sugar Mill Ruins State Historic Site, page 33.

SEMINOLES AND THE SEMINOLE WARS

Seminoles had little reason to like the Americans, who wanted them removed first from certain areas of Florida, and then removed from the entire state. American forces throughout the southeastern U.S. had battled Creeks from whom the Seminoles derived for many years before there were Seminoles in Florida. The Florida Seminoles included African Americans, many of whom had escaped into the sparsely populated Peninsula, even before Florida became American territory in 1821.

Andrew Jackson, a future president and the first military governor, was famed for his role in the Creek Wars, and later led American forces to victory in the First Seminole War. Jackson was merciless in efforts against Native Americans in general. The Creeks and Seminoles at various times sided with British and Spanish forces against the U.S.

Three wars between the Seminoles and U.S. forces are generally given in these time spans: First Seminole War, 1817-1818; Second Seminole War, 1835-1842; and Third Seminole War, 1855-1858. In reality, there were skirmishes and disputes between the Seminoles and Americans before and during the entire period and beyond. The First Seminole War can be thought of in terms of an attack on Seminoles living in Spanish Florida, while the Second and Third Seminole Wars were largely attempts to remove the Seminoles from certain areas within Florida and from Florida itself.

The Seminoles derived from various groups of the Creek peoples. Even in modern times, Seminoles do not possess one single language but represent various cultural and linguistic backgrounds.

The origin of the name "Seminole" is uncertain and is not without some disagreement. One linguist gives a Creek naming of *Sim-in-oli,* meaning wild. The Spanish called them *Cimarones,* wild people. *Place Names of Florida* cites the Creek name as *ishti semoli,* wild men; or the origin as the Spanish *Cimarron,* wild or unruly.

In present times, we know the Seminole Tribe for its gambling casinos and ownership of the chain, Hard Rock Cafes. The present-day Seminole Tribe of Florida has come a long way since hiding in the swamps from America's merciless soldiers. Today's tribe employs over 2,000 non-Indians and purchases 24 million dollars in goods and services from a variety of non-Indian vendors. The tribe operates four gaming facilities at Coconut Grove, Hollywood, Immokalee, and Tampa, bringing tourists and revenues to the Sunshine State. There are five reservations: Big Cypress, Brighton, Fort Pierce, Hollywood, and Tampa.

▲ *Seminole leader Osceola was imprisoned at Ft. Moultrie in South Carolina where he died in 1838.*

△ *Seminole alligator wrestlers put on a show for tourists.*

AH-TAH-THI-KY MUSEUM
(Collier and Hendry counties)

Two museums of this name are operated by the Seminole Tribe of Florida. Meaning "a place to learn," an impressive museum sits beside a 60-acre cypress dome and 1-mile boardwalk at the Seminole Indian Reservation of Big Cypress National Park. A second museum is located with the Seminole Hard Rock Hotel and Casino in Hollywood. Both museums have rare artifacts and educational exhibits. Special tours can be arranged, and the museums are open daily, except for holidays. To reach the museum located in the Big Cypress, take I-75 west (northbound) from Miami and exit north on CR-833. Proceed to Boundary Road and follow the signs.

BULOW PLANTATION RUINS STATE HISTORIC STATE PARK
(Flagler and Volusia counties)

Bulow Plantation was the largest sugar mill in territorial East Florida in the 1830s. The Sugar Mill Ruins are currently listed on the National Register of Historic Places. In 1821, Major Charles William Bulow acquired 4,675 acres of wilderness along a tidal creek near Ormond Beach. Bulow's days were numbered, but before he died a year later at age 44, he established a plantation worked by slaves. Here he planted rice, indigo, sugar cane, and cotton. His son John carried on after his father's death but not before traveling to Paris for his education. In 1831, fate brought James John Audubon to Bulow where he reported in correspondence "a most hospitable and welcome treatment." Bulow was opposed to the U.S. government's treatment of the Seminole Indians at this time and its commitment to dispossess them of their Florida lands and to send them to reservations west of the Mississippi. For a time, Bulow was held captive by U.S. troops. It is ironic that Seminoles burned his plantation to the ground in 1836 during a raid. From I-95, take Exit 90 east to CR-2001 (Old Kings Highway Road). A prominent sign directs visitors to Plantation Road, the original entrance to Bulow Plantation.

△ *Seminole lady gathering saw palmetto leaves for basket making. Big Cypress Reservation, 1980.*

DADE BATTLEFIELD HISTORIC STATE PARK (Sumter County)

On December 28th, 1835, a contingent of 107 soldiers led by Brevet Major Francis Dade was ambushed by a superior force of Seminole warriors near the present-day town of Bushnell. En route from Tampa's Ft. Brooke, Dade and his men were bound for Ft. King, a primitive log stockade near what is now downtown Ocala. The men were tired; they'd been on the march for three days. Because most Indian skirmishes had previously occurred in the swamp, the soldiers were unprepared for an attack in the pine forest. The Seminole assault was sudden and devastating. Dade's men fought desperately, firing a cannon to keep the Indians at bay while they constructed breastwork. Once the soldiers had run out of powder, the end came swiftly. Only two soldiers (Privates Ransom Clark and Joseph Sprague) survived to tell of their defeat. Clark retired from the Army and went on the lecture circuit, so to speak, for several years until he died from an unspecified illness. Sprague continued in the service and lived out his normal life. At the time it was the worst loss ever suffered by the U.S. Army at the hands of Native Americans, exceeded only by George Armstrong Custer's disastrous last stand at Little Bighorn some 41 years later. The Dade Massacre marked the beginning of the Second Seminole War (1835-1842), the longest and most costly Indian conflict ever fought by the country. Each year, on the weekend closest to December 28th, members of the Dade Battlefield Society camp at the park and reenact the massacre before an audience of several thousand delighted visitors. The event includes live demonstrations and a trade fair. Prizes are awarded for the most historically accurate costumes and campsites. From I-75, north of Tampa, exit east on SR-48.

FORT CHRISTMAS HISTORICAL PARK (Orange County)

On December 25, 1837, during the Second Seminole Indian War, U.S. soldiers and volunteers arrived at this spot near the St. Johns River to construct a military supply depot. Abandoned by the following spring, the aptly named fort eventually fell into disrepair. In 1976, as part of a bicentennial project, a replica was constructed 1 mile south of the original fort. Today, the 25-acre county park features restored pioneer homes and farming equipment from the 1870s to the early 1900s. The historical park, located at the intersection of SR-50 and Fort Christmas Road, includes picnic tables, playgrounds, and free museum admission. From I-95, take exit 215 west

⋀ Seminole male (1900s). After the wars of the 1800s, the remaining Seminole peoples moved into the then-unpopulated South Florida, where they lived in relative isolation for several decades.

toward Orlando and merge onto Cheney Highway/SR-50. Continue on SR-50 west for approximately 10 miles and turn right at South Fort Christmas Road.

FORT COOPER STATE PARK (Citrus County)

In 1836 a Major Cooper, for whom the park is named, was given orders to establish a site to care for sick and wounded soldiers. Cooper was given sufficient men for the task; five companies of the First Georgia Battalion of Engineers and an artillery company. A company usually consists of 61 to a 190 soldiers, more or less, usually commanded by a captain. A structure was erected on the banks of Lake Holathlikaha. Several fights took place there during the Second Seminole War. The structure has been recreated. In addition to the history, canoes can be rented and the lake paddled, and there are excellent hiking trails – 6.2 miles. The park is several miles south of Inverness and an east turn from US-41. Well-placed signs announce the turn.

FORT FOSTER STATE HISTORIC SITE (Hillsborough County)

Part of the Florida park system, the site includes a replica fort from the Second Seminole War. The site's interpretive center displays artifacts of the fort, Florida pioneering life, and the Seminole Wars. Annual reenactments are conducted in late February. The sites of Fort Alabama and Foster were erected in the same location to defend a bridge that allowed the Fort King Military Road to cross the Hillsborough River. Fort Alabama was established in 1836 and abandoned a few months later, and destroyed by a likely booby trap that exploded when the troops were departing. Fort Foster was established in 1836 and abandoned in 1838 because of repeated sickness. The site was added to the National Register of Historic Places in 1972 and is located in Thonotosassa at 15402 US-301, across the highway from Hillsborough River State Park. Although the site is not open daily, guided tours and group events are available through the Florida Park Service.

INDIAN KEY HISTORIC STATE PARK
(Monroe County)

Just a quarter mile off Lower Matecumbe on the Atlantic side, the small island of Indian Key offers visitors a haunting glimpse of the hopes and dreams of two of the Florida Keys' interesting pioneers. Indian Key was purchased in 1831 by Jacob Housman. He proceeded to build houses, streets, cisterns, a town square, a hotel, a general store, a blacksmith shop, and a wharf. In 1836, he persuaded the state to designate the island the Official Seat of Dade County. By the late 1830s, Indian Key was home to at least 40 permanent residents, including Dr. Henry Perrine, a physician and prominent amateur botanist. On August 7, 1840, the islanders were attacked by a group of Seminole Indians. Although most escaped, Dr. Perrine was killed, and every structure on Indian Key was burnt to the ground. Today, only the cisterns and stone foundations remain. Jacob Housman died the following year, crushed between two boat hulls during a salvage operation on rough seas. The island is open to the public from sunrise to sunset. Visitors can rent a kayak at a marina located at Mile Marker 77.5 on the bayside. The kayak trip takes about 45 minutes. It is best to go early before the afternoon winds pick up.

OKEECHOBEE BATTLEFIELD/ JONATHAN DICKINSON STATE PARK
(Okeechobee and Martin counties)

On Christmas Day, 1837, approximately 800 troops commanded by Zachary Taylor did battle with approximately 400 opposing Seminoles during the Second Seminole War. The Seminole forces were led by Billy Bowlegs (there have been several Seminole leaders named Billy Bowlegs). Both sides claimed victory, but the Americans must have been convinced their side won, since they promoted "Old Rough and Ready" to the rank of general. In 2006, Florida purchased the land where the battle is thought to have taken place. A reenactment takes place with volunteers. The land is managed as of this writing by Jonathan Dickinson State Park.

PAYNES CREEK HISTORIC STATE PARK
(Hardee County)

Fort Chokonikla, originally built in the summer of 1849 as an inland outpost for the sole purpose of keeping the Seminoles in check, was located on this site. Fort Chokonikla was one in a systematic group of forts built throughout Florida. The only warriors who attacked this fort, however, were a pesky onslaught of mosquitoes. Today visitors may learn about the Fort Chokonikla site and the Kennedy-Darling Trading Post site from a lookout perch over Payne's Creek; a monument there is a testament to Captain George S. Payne, Dempsey Whiddon, and employees of the Dempsey-Darling Trading Post who lost their lives in an attack by five renegade Indians. Found objects and artifacts recovered from the area may be viewed at the visitor center as well as an interpretive presentation of the historical significance of the site. The park is located to the east of the small town of Bowling Green, south of Bartow on US-17. From US-17, turn east on CR664-A, which leads to the park.

SETTLER LIFE

During the European period, settlements occurred primarily along coastal areas, at ports, and in the Keys. In Florida's early years as an American territory, most settlers were attracted to the rich lands in "Middle Florida," the area around present-day Tallahassee. The growth into the new frontier was spurred by the establishment of Florida as a territory and by a steady and rapid migration.

During settler times, the north of Florida was populated most quickly at first, perhaps because it is more moderate in climate and fertile ground for cotton, naval stores, and lumbering. The state slowly filled out southward along the coasts, in places such as Cedar Key, while the center of Florida became primarily cattle land, an industry that still thrives. The settlers came mostly in wagons from the eastern part of the U.S. and the adjacent south, but some settlers came from farther afield. Many settlers brought slaves.

Unlike most states east of the Mississippi River, Florida remained a frontier long into the late-nineteenth and early twentieth centuries. Oppressive heat, lack of transportation facilities, and other obstacles made for harsh living conditions until the advent of air-conditioning and mosquito control. In 1825, Florida held more than 10,000 settlers; five years later, the number exceeded 15,000. By 1840, almost 35,000 settlers are believed to have been in Florida. By the beginning of the Civil War in 1861, about 140,000 lived in Florida; about half of these were enslaved African Americans.

Many of the white settlers, particularly the ones who relocated from south and southeast, were referred to as "Crackers," a term presently revered by some and pejorative to others. The term is still used to describe white, rural, native Floridians.

The origin of the word Cracker is not clear. There are three common theories: they "cracked corn" to make bread or meal, they cracked whips while driving cattle, and cracked boasts or jokes. In fact, Samuel Johnson's famous 18th century dictionary defined a "cracker" as a noisy boisterous fellow. These were mostly Scotch-Irish folk and brought with them to the American frontier the positive (and negative) traits typical of their backgrounds.

The Crackers were resourceful, self-sufficient, independent, and determined to live life free of restraints. They squatted on unclaimed lands, grew corn, and herded cattle and pigs, built "shotgun cabins" (structures seemingly thrown together), fished, hunted, procreated, and survived -- no mean task on one of America's roughest frontiers. A significant inducement to immigration in Florida occurred in 1842 after the Second Seminole War when Congress passed the Armed Occupation Act, which allowed homesteaders to stake claim to 160 acres in the Lower Peninsula. Five years of consecutive occupation granted settlers title to the lands free and clear. But making a go of it in this harsh Florida environment was hard for men and women alike. Some prospered more than others, but those that survived created a livelihood and culture that sustained them during the hard times. Crackers have left a mark on Florida that is still felt today.

ADDISON BLOCKHOUSE HISTORIC STATE PARK **(Volusia County)**

In the early days, Florida's blockhouses were built as a means of defending settlers from Native Americans. Later, blockhouses were used during the Seminole wars. The thick, fortified walls of the Addison Blockhouse were made from a mixture of lime, sand, and shell forming impenetrable walls known as tabby. The house is located in Tomoka State Park on a bend in the Tomoka River. The Addison Blockhouse is a vestige of a 19th century rice-and-sugar plantation owned by John Addison. The plantation existed from 1816 until 1856 on 20,000 acres, until burned by Native Americans. During the early Florida economy the plantation became a sugar processing operation with a steam-powered sugar mill. This historic site is not accessible to the public as of this writing. However, ongoing preservation of the blockhouse will eventually allow it to be open for tours. Tomoka State Park is located 3 miles north of Ormond Beach on North Beach Street.

BELLEVUE (Leon County)

Prince Achille Murat lived at Bellevue with his American princess, Catherine Willis Gray. They named Bellevue for a hotel in Brussels of which they had fond memories. Princess Murat was a great-grandniece of George Washington, while the Prince was a son of the King of Naples and a nephew of Napoleon. Catherine was involved with efforts to preserve Mount Vernon, Washington's home. Bellevue ("pretty view") was built in 1831 by Samuel DuVal (a nephew of Governor DuVal); Samuel originally built the house for Ellen Willis, his bride and sister of the princess.

The Murats moved into the structure in the 1820s. Bellevue was later the home at one time of Governor Bloxham. The lands were operated as a plantation, and Bellevue is often referred to as Bellevue Plantation. On the cusp of the Civil War, Bellevue consisted of a number of buildings, 470 acres, and possessed 24 slaves. It is located off SR-371 south of Tallahassee. The house was placed on the National Register of Historic Places in 1971. Tallahassee possesses a Bellevue Way, a Bellevue Middle School, and a roadway bypassing Tallahassee known as the Bloxham Cutoff. The Murats are buried at St. Johns Episcopal Cemetery on Call Street within the city limits of Tallahassee. Bloxham served two non-consecutive terms as governor: 1881-1885 and 1897-1901. The Gov. W. D. Bloxham House is located at 410 North Calhoun Street. Bloxham was a public servant who held many offices but who is best remembered today for founding Florida A&M University.

⋀ *Governor William Bloxham, 1900.*

⋀ *A view of the period kitchen at Cedar Keys State Museum.*

CEDAR KEYS STATE MUSEUM
(Levy County)

Within the museum is an excellent collection of artifacts, including awesome arrowheads and spear points unearthed from the mounds of early Timucuans who lived in the area. The centerpiece of the park, however, is the restored home of St. Clair Whitman, a collector of butterflies, a collector of historical photographs of the area, and a collector of seashells. The house is an excellent example of what it was like to live in Florida at the turn of the 20th century. Whitman and his father moved to the Cedar Key area when his mother died in 1880. He worked at various forms of employment in the area, including the Eagle Pencil Company, and survived the hurricane of 1896 that ended the pencil industry. From US-19 between Crystal River and Chiefland, turn west on SR-24. Near the city of Cedar Key the turns to the state park are clearly announced by signs. The park is not open every day of the week, and it would be wise to check the operating schedule before venturing a trip.

ᗐ *A replica of John Gorrie's ice machine on view at the John Gorrie Museum.*

EDEN GARDENS STATE PARK
(Santa Rosa County)

Did you happen to catch the 1972 film *The Frogs* staring movie legend Ray Milland? The B-movie horror flick paralleled Hitchcock's *The Birds*, only it was filled with poisonous amphibians imported to attack local residents. This film was made at Eden Gardens. There is nothing to fear, as beauty and solitude fill the 160-acre gardens, not demonic frogs. The centerpiece is the 5,500 square-foot Wesley House. Around it are camellia and azalea gardens, a hidden garden, a butterfly garden, a reflective pool, and oaks 500-600 years old. Normally camellias and azaleas bloom near the beginning of spring presenting a colorful spectacle. The current house appears to be antebellum, but is in fact an original 1896 Victorian building reworked into a 1963 Greek-revival mansion. To the east of Destin, signs announce the turn to the gardens from US-98 onto SR-395 in Port Washington.

GOODWOOD PLANTATION (Leon County)

One of North Florida's most historic properties, Goodwood Plantation, now Goodwood Museum and Gardens, was part of the Marquis de LaFayette land grant of the 1820s. Through a succession of owners, Goodwood parallels the history of North Florida and Leon County from the plantation days of the 19th century, through the quail-hunting country estate days of the early 20th century, to the shift in the 1940s from an agricultural to a political and service-based economy. Visitors come to Goodwood to see the heirloom rose gardens or the tens of thousands of daffodils planted in "bulb lawns," a very popular way to plant bulbs in the 1800s but rarely seen today. The Main House, an elegant home with frescoed ceilings in the front parlor, houses Goodwood's museum collection, which rivals those seen in cities renowned as Southern historic and cultural centers: Charleston, Natchez, New Orleans, and Savannah. Goodwood, located in the heart of Tallahassee at 1600 Miccosukee Road, has a history rich with stories that span from the 1830s to the 1990s. (Account provided by Goodwood Museum and Gardens) From I-10, take Capital Circle South for several miles, then turn west on Miccosukee Road. A brown sign announces the turn.

JOHN GORRIE MUSEUM STATE PARK
(Franklin County)

John Gorrie was a resident of Apalachicola and developed an ice-making machine in the 1840s. Believe it or not, ice was harvested in the north and shipped south at great expense. Gorrie's ice method led to the making of ice in hot climates. Most of the readers of this book are too young to remember a Florida without air-conditioning or with an icebox. Until the mid-1950s, however, air-condition was a miracle reserved for restaurants, movie theaters, and the occasional home of the wealthy. Gorrie, however, was not interested in ice for cocktails or air-conditioning for the rich when he made his invention. Gorrie was a physician trying to save yellow fever patients in the early 1800s from their deadly-high body temperatures. The Museum lies along US-98 in the City of Apalachicola. Also of interest in Apalachicola is the Ormond House, once owned by another physician. Check the museum hours of operation before making a visit.

GREGORY HOUSE/TORREYA STATE PARK (Liberty County)

Torreya State Park is mostly known for its biological marvels. Located on cliffs overlooking the Apalachicola River, Torreya includes vanishing trees, like its namesake Torreya and the Florida yew, copperheads, a tiny waterfall, gorgeous and challenging hiking trails, and overnight camping. It also includes a plantation-style house that was moved from the other side of the river by the Civilian Conservation Corps in the 1930s. Torreya was one of many state parks created by the CCC. From I-10 west of Tallahassee, exit on SR-12 and follow the signs to CR-1641. That road leads into Torreya State Park.

HERITAGE VILLAGE (Pinellas County)

Originally conceived of in the year of the Bi-Centennial, Heritage Village opened in 1977 funded by the Pinellas Board of County Commissioners. It is also supported by: the Pinellas County Historical Society, Pin-Mar, an antique car club, and other community groups. Starting with four historic buildings and 10 acres, Heritage Village today comprises 21 acres with over 25 structures to illustrate the story of Pinellas history through time. Most of the buildings missed a date with the wrecking ball. Collectively, the buildings represent life in Pinellas from the Civil War through the 1930s. A ramble through the shaded pine forest on a serpentine brick walkway reveals everything from an 1850s log house, a railroad depot, a red caboose, a church, a one-room school house, to an early mercantile store, a 1920s service garage, all capped off with a couple of over-the-hill outhouses, and a sugar-cane grinding mill. Costumed, docent-led tours are available through some of the houses, or one might just want to strikeout on a self-guided tour. The centerpiece of the park is the two-phase Pinellas County Historical Museum separated by an old fashioned dogtrot (breezeway) to capture the cooling wind. The Pinellas Historical Society provides historical and cultural programs throughout the year. The research museum at Heritage provides a valuable resource for other county historical societies and to the general public at large. From US-19, proceed west on Ulmerton Road (SR-688). Turn south on 125th Street North and signs will show the way.

HOMELAND HERITAGE PARK (Polk County)

Included on the 5-acre site are the Homeland School (1878), the old Hometown Methodist Church (1880), the Raulerson House (1880), and log cabins and a barn (1888). These buildings and exhibits offer insight to the world of homesteaders. From SR-60 east of Bartow, go south on US-98/17 to Homeland Garfield Road and turn west.

MICANOPY HISTORICAL DISTRICT & HISTORICAL SOCIETY MUSEUM (Alachua County)

Micanopy was as close to a "head chief" as the loosely affiliated Seminoles had during the period of the Second Seminole War. Like Osceola, Micanopy was taken prisoner under a flag of truce. The town of Micanopy is the longest-settled town inland in Florida. It has perhaps one of the most unaltered, pristine historic districts in an ever-changing, fast-growing, modern-day Sunshine State. Micanopy (pronounced Mick-can-oh'-pee) was known variously as Cuscowilla and Wantons. It became Micanopy not long after Moses Levy settled the area soon after Florida became an American territory. Fittingly, the museum has displays from the Seminoles as well as settler and Civil War days. Included in the items on display is a Sibley Tent Stove, a type of stove used in tents for heat; it was salvaged from a grove where it provided warmth during freezes. From I-75, take C-.234 off I-75 south of Gainesville; this is the first exit south of Gainesville. Drive 1 mile east of the Interstate to the downtown.

⋏ A salt kettle at Cedar Keys State Museum. In the days before refrigeration, pork, beef, and fish were packed in salt to prevent spoiling during shipment and storage. Salt was produced by boiling sea water in kettles like this. As the water boiled away, salt was left. This kettle is one of 60 that produced 150 bushels of salt a day at the Cedar Key Confederate salt works, which was destroyed by a Union raiding party in October 1862.

On the eve of the Civil War in 1861, the relatively small population (140,000 total, of whom perhaps 60-65,000 were slaves) of Florida was clustered about a few towns: Apalachicola, Cedar Key, Fernandina, Jacksonville, Key West, Tampa, Pensacola, and St. Augustine. This was a population density of about 2 per square mile, greatly less in the wilderness, highly more around the cities, and obviously there were great gaps in-between those cities and lesser towns. Most hostile actions in Florida during the Civil War concerned cattle, salt making, and control of the ports mentioned above.

To the soldiers who died during the Civil War and to their families, Florida's role surely seemed significant. From a broader view, however, Florida's place in the war was somewhat peripheral.

Florida's greatest impact in the Civil War may not have been in military clashes or in the number of its sons who fought largely for the Confederacy. Rather, think cattle and salt, food and preservatives. In the times of the Civil War, slaughtered beef was preserved using salt. Salt beef and salt pork were the provisions on which armies moved, and after the fall of Vicksburg in July 1863, the hungry Confederate armies turned to Florida for beef. Always a little confused about itself, Florida supplied cattle and salt to both sides in the Civil War and at times tricked both sides also. In the ruthless world of "root hog or die," South Florida, frontier folk often decided their best chances came with the side with cash. Union gold often trumped depreciated Confederate paper. Support for secession was most pronounced in the "Middle Florida" plantation belt. There was much Union sentiment in Florida, especially among the cattle-producing areas in the Lower Peninsula. It could perhaps be stated that these folk were more anti-Confederate than they were Unionist. Substantial isolated pockets on Florida resisted Confederate conscription and impressments of supplies. Some "laid out" in the swamps and forests. Others served in the few Union units that operated out of Ft. Myers, Jacksonville, and Pensacola.

It is reported that up and down the Florida coasts at night fires were burning during the conflict. These fires were not for navigation, and most lighthouses were disabled, the lenses destroyed or carted off. The fires burned to boil down salt from the sea. The saltwater was boiled in giant, iron kettles. A photograph of such a kettle from Cedar Key appears with this text. Key West fell into Union hands from the outset of the war and provided a base for the Gulf Coast Blockading Squadron. Union raids on Ft. Myers, Tampa Bay, and Cedar Key continually disrupted salt-making efforts.

Florida largely escaped significant battles during the Civil War because the Confederate shortage of soldiers caused it to "write off" the state and move most troops north almost immediately. The Union forces dallied in Florida for a while longer. Lincoln had considered the forts around Pensacola vital to the efforts, but this belief may not have made tactical sense. (Indeed, the so-called "first shot" was fired at Fort Sumter in Charleston rather than at Fort Pickens in Pensacola.) Later, when Grant took command of Union forces, he essentially did the same thing as the Confederates, writing Florida off and concentrating on Lee's army. Sherman's devastating "March to the Sea" concentrated on Georgia and the Carolinas, leaving Florida unscathed. But Union armies occupied Jacksonville numerous times, and withdrawing Confederates torched the city every time. Near the end of the war Union forces (with black troops in their ranks) raided south from Jacksonville along the St. Johns, wreaking havoc wherever they went, and fleeing "contrabands" joined them whenever they could.

Sixteen thousand Floridians were conscripted into Confederate forces largely to fight elsewhere. They fought in faraway battlefields in Mississippi, Tennessee, and Alabama. Florida regiments fought in Robert E. Lee's Army of Northern Virginia. Many of those men survived the war to lay down their arms at Appomattox Courthouse. Drawing 16,000 men largely from a white population of less than 80,000 left the state financially handicapped and made the war a hardship, although a different kind than suffered throughout the rest of the South.

While significant skirmishes between Yankees and Confederates took place in Marianna, Natural Bridge (south of Tallahassee), and in raids along the St. Johns, the only pitched battle in Florida involving large numbers of troops took place in the woods about Olustee, near present-day Lake City. It was a sort of accident that the battle happened and the loss drove the Union forces back to about Jacksonville, a considerable distance. After that, Union efforts in Florida were minor in number and effect. The operation at Olustee was undertaken as an attempt by Union forces to sever the trade in beef and salt. A victory for the Confederacy, the casualties were comparatively staggering on both sides. The union force of 5,500 soldiers took 1,353 casualties, about a quarter of its force, including 203 killed in action. Confederates took nearly 1,000 casualties, with 93 killed. This defeat was made possible because the Union forces were trapped in a small natural funnel of land where Confederate troops, having been forewarned, lay in ambush.

Florida Governor John Milton like many Southerners was unable to bear the loss to the Union. Milton, a plantation owner from Jackson County, took his life in shotgun blast in Marianna in 1865 shortly after the war was lost.

Florida was greatly disrupted by the Civil War and ensuing defeat. This disruption took place in the strained lives of its populace in the man-depleted war years and continued through the upheaval of Reconstruction, a period of economic and political change. Most importantly, the war brought freedom to the former slaves.

Much is made of the fact that Tallahassee was the only unconquered state capitol in the south. This was due to the Battle of Olustee and Natural Bridge, fought in the winter of 1864. This may be much to do about nothing, as there was not much strategic value to capturing the city. Union and Confederate forces clashed elsewhere deciding the war. If either side had captured Tallahassee, its impact on the war would have been small at best and perhaps nil.

CIVIL WAR DISCOVERY TRAIL (Statewide)

This historic trail is the creation of The Civil War Preservation Trust, with help from the National Park Service, The National Trust for Historic Preservation, and state and local governments. It includes more than 600 sites in 32 states, including Florida, and is growing. Contact information can be obtained from Appendix A under Civil War Discovery Trail.

FORT BARRANCAS, FORT McREE, AND FORT PICKENS, GULF ISLANDS NATIONAL SEASHORE (Escambia County)

The first shots fired in the Civil War are believed by some to be those of January 8, 1861, when forces sympathetic to the Confederacy tried to take Fort Barrancas (although the vast majority of historians believe the incident on the bridge at Fort Barrancas was minor). Before long, Fort Pickens was under siege and Forts Barrancas and McRee had been abandoned. When Confederate forces took much of this area in 1861, there were bombardments from two Union vessels, although most of the firing was from Fort Pickens, one of only four Southern forts not taken by Confederate forces. Fort Pickens is the largest fort that defended Pensacola Harbor and Naval Yard. It is located on the western tip of Santa Rosa Island. The Apache leader Geronimo was brought to Fort Pickens in the 1880s and held prisoner. Portions of Gulf Islands National Seashore can be reached from Pensacola by following US-98 across Pensacola Bay, then taking SR-399 onto Santa Rosa Island, and turning west once on the island. It is best to check in advance of the trip with Gulf Islands National Seashore as portions of the island have at times been rendered hard to access due to storms.

FORT CLINCH STATE PARK (Nassau County)

Today Fort Clinch is a wonderful place to walk along the Atlantic Ocean or kayak in the Amelia River. It is a favorite camping spot and has fine hiking and bicycling trails and a long stretch of Atlantic beach. When it was built before the Civil War, the fort sat in a strategic location, at the mouth of the St. Marys River. Its role in the Civil War, however, was marginal. It was seized by Confederate troops in 1861 and abandoned to Federal troops the following year. It is, however, wonderfully preserved, and it is a rewarding experience to tour the old fort. From I-95 south of the Georgia border, exit east on A-1A, and head north with A1A once on Amelia Island.

⩒ *Fort Clinch State Park*

JUDAH P. BENJAMIN

During the Civil War, Judah P. Benjamin was at various times the Confederate Attorney General, Secretary of State, and Secretary of War. The former Louisiana Senator was a close associate of Jefferson Davis who called him "my most trusted confidante." At war's end, they remained together only briefly, parting ways on May 3, 1865. Hell-bent on eluding Union capture Benjamin disguised himself as a French Journalist named "M. Bonfal." He moved furtively and hid with sympathetic Confederate families. From Tampa, Judah found his way to the Gamble Plantation where he knew safety could be found at the residence of Archibald McNeil, Deputy Commissary of the Manatee District of the Confederacy. A $40,000 Union bounty placed upon Benjamin drove him to continue his journey by boat to Bimini by way of Sarasota on July 10, 1865. Judah P. Benjamin ultimately landed in London on August 30, 1865, and went on to become a noted barrister achieving great financial success. Highly respected by the House of Lords, a fall off a tram finally short-circuited his health. He rejoined his wife in retirement in Paris where he died in 1884.

GAMBLE PLANTATION HISTORIC STATE PARK (Manatee County)

The last thing one would expect to find traveling south on I-75 after passing the Ellenton Outlet Mall would be an authentic, antebellum home reminiscent of Charleston, but near there is located the Gamble Plantation. It is the oldest building on the West Coast of Florida and the southernmost plantation in the nation. With its front gable and 18 massive columns wrapping the front and side façades, the Gamble Mansion is a classic example of antebellum construction. Built between 1845 and 1850 by Major Robert Gamble of Tallahassee, the slave-operated plantation grew to a total of 3,500 acres. At its peak, the plantation boasted production of up to 1,500 hogshead of refined sugar annually. Don't know what a hogshead is? Don't feel bad, as not many people use this term any longer. A hogshead is a large barrel of liquid, usually 63 gallons, sometimes more. From I-75, take the Ellenton exit (US-301) and follow the signs.

NATURAL BRIDGE BATTLEFIELD HISTORIC STATE PARK (Wakulla County)

The Battle of Natural Bridge that prevented Union forces from marching on Tallahassee was fought on March 7, 1864, and resulted in Union losses of 21 killed and 89 wounded versus Confederate losses of 3 killed and 22 wounded. Confederate troops, commanded by General William Miller, were a rag-tag collection of Tallahassee volunteers, local boys, and old men. Their victory over seasoned Union forces (commanded by Commander William Gibson) has a mythic David versus Goliath element. The Union forces were essentially forced to cross on a natural bridge, which limited their maneuverability. The bridge is an area of land between springs where water goes underground, not infrequent in northern Florida. The locals were familiar with the natural bridge; the invaders were not. From Tallahassee, proceed south on SR-363 and turn east on CR-2192, which dead-ends at Natural Bridge Battlefield Historic State Park.

OLUSTEE BATTLEFIELD HISTORIC STATE PARK (Baker County)

Olustee is 10-15 minutes east of Lake City and in the heart of Osceola National Forrest. It is difficult to imagine that a battle involving several thousand soldiers took place in such a quiet locale without witnessing the Olustee Battle re-enacted. Roughly one-third of the Union troops were African Americans, mostly composed of elements of the famed 54th Massachusetts (depicted in the movie "Glory"). White

⋏ *Gamble Plantation, current era.*

⋏ *Civil War reenactment at Olustee Battlefield.*

soldiers were from Connecticut, New Hampshire, New York, and Massachusetts. Two-thirds of the Confederate forces were Georgians. From I-75 in Lake City, go east on US-90 to Olustee.

YULEE SUGAR MILLS HISTORIC STATE PARK (Citrus County)

David Levy Yulee (June 12, 1810 to October 10, 1886) was the first practicing Jew to become a member of the U.S. Senate when the Florida legislature selected him as one of its first Senators in 1845. From 1851 to 1864, Yulee owned a successful sugar plantation named Margarita that was located on Tiger Tail Island on the Homosassa River. It was 5,000 acres and worked by 1,000 slaves. When the Civil War came along, Yulee's sympathies were with the Southern cause, and the mill became a major supplier to the Confederacy. This cost Yulee, however, as after the war he endured a brief confinement in a Union prison at Fort Pulaski. The sugar mill fell into ruin after the Civil War. However, enough vestiges remained of the mill works to become a Florida historic site. Extant today are a limestone-hewn chimney, gears from the old machinery, and a sugarcane press. The park is located in the small town of Homosassa, which is located about 3 miles west of the city of Homosassa Springs. Take US-19 to the town of Homosassa Springs, then turn west onto CR-490 West (Yulee Drive). Proceed for approximately 2.5 miles to the park.

"Reconstruct 1. To construct again; rebuild; makeover." – Webster's

⌃ *Congressman Josiah Walls, 1873.*

Reconstruction is defined by the decade following the Civil War, in which the federal government attempted to enforce in full measure the 14th and 15th Amendments (black equality and voting rights for blacks in the Southern states). Florida shares the distinction with Louisiana and South Carolina as the last three Southern states to be "redeemed," that is, restored to white Democratic rule after a period of Republican state government. On a national level, it was a very turbulent period, perhaps the most turbulent except for the Civil War itself. President Lincoln, who appeared to have had a vision of how the U.S. would be put back together, died at the hands of John Wilkes Booth in Ford's Theater; whatever Lincoln's vision may have been, it died with him. Lincoln's successor Andrew Johnson, a Southerner, battled with Congressional leaders committed to black equality and voting rights and sought to obstruct Congress and moderate the harsh conditions imposed on the South. In this, he failed, and over it, he barely survived a vote of impeachment.

In Florida, much the same sort of bitter political struggle occurred between Republicans, many recently moved to the state, and Conservative-Democrats (who largely represented the white property owners) and former Confederates (who were not only defeated and impoverished, but who felt oppressed). The two political sides contested in scandalous, often illegal ways (including murder), over the power to govern the state. In the end, it was the forces of the old Confederacy that came to dominate Florida with the close of Reconstruction.

During Reconstruction, Florida elected one of the first seven black members of Congress, Representative Josiah Walls. Representative Walls was a vigorous champion of civil rights and education for all. He had been born into slavery in Virginia, and his father is believed to have been the slaveholder. During the Civil War, Josiah Walls fought in a "colored" unit of the U.S. Army reaching the rank of corporal. He was discharged in Florida and settled in Alachua County. Josiah was apparently a powerful speaker, and in time he came to own and publish "The New Era" newspaper in Gainesville. Walls served not only in Congress, but he was also in the state senate.

Suffering in this power struggle were the largely powerless former slaves, who were alternatively protected by the occupation troops and mistreated at every step toward full civil rights. In the beginning, the African Americans did not have the vote. Then when they were franchised, they were hit with a poll tax, which virtually excluded them from exercising their vote. As freedmen, the majority of the former slaves (along with a large number of poor whites) became caught in an oppressive system of peonage known as sharecropping. The system was an economic reality in the "New South" and stunted opportunities of Florida's poor.

While Florida, with the exception of Jacksonville, did not take the brunt of physical devastation wrought on the South, it was a land in limbo. Some lands were confiscated from Confederate supporters and doled out to Unionists by the occupying army, then later given back to the old landowners by President Johnson. There was no government at the end of the war—only military occupation. The Confederate currency was valueless, and with property in slaves written off the books, land values plummeted. Many lost their land for non-payment of taxes.

The term "The Gilded Age" comes from a book Mark Twain co-authored with Charles Dudley Warner, a writer who, alas, has faded into time and out of print (the worst possible fate for a writer, except death), unlike (Samuel Clements) Mark Twain. The term "Gilded Age" refers to post-Reconstruction America, a period of rampant corruption. In "Gilded Age" Florida, the state's transportation system, such as it was, was largely non-operational because Florida's broken down railroads were crippled by debt and injunctions. With Florida debt heavy and transportation practically non-existent, Florida's "redeemer" politicians sought to lure out-of-state investors with gifts of tax exemptions and land giveaways. A case in point is the deal that Gov. William Bloxham worked out in 1884 with Philadelphia tool-and-dye industrialist Hamilton Disston to sell him four million acres of land for $.25 per acre (virtually all of South Florida).

In 1884, after the Supreme Court ruled the 1875 Civil Rights Act unconstitutional, Florida, along with most other Southern states, moved to re-write its constitution. The new constitution abrogated the 1868 one, limited the power of the governor, and provided for election of Florida cabinet members and members of the Florida Supreme Court. When the constitution was ratified in 1889, only 24 years after Lincoln's death, black Floridians were effectively disenfranchised.

DEBARY HALL HISTORIC SITE
(Volusia County)

The years following the Civil War dramatically transformed Florida as northern travelers embraced improvements in rail and water transportation. One such visitor was wine merchant and steamboat mogul Frederick DeBary. Enamored with Central Florida's exotic landscape, DeBary constructed a hunting lodge and wintering retreat in 1871. A massive staff was required to tend to the endless stream of famous and wealthy guests, as well as maintaining the enormous estate and 8,000 square-foot house at 210 Sunrise Boulevard. Today, the 10-acre DeBary Hall Historic Site offers programs, exhibits, and artifacts on DeBary and the late 19th century men and women in the St. Johns River region. From I-4, take Exit 108 and turn right on Dirksen Drive. Turn right on Mansion Boulevard and left on Sunrise Boulevard.

HARRIET BEECHER STOWE HOUSE
(Duval County)

Just south of Jacksonville Naval Air Station on a wide stretch of the St. Johns River is the charming community of Mandarin. Home to several wintering poets and artists, Mandarin's most famous resident was Harriet Beecher Stowe. She was an early civil-rights champion and author of the famous novel *Uncle Tom's Cabin*.

It was here in the early 1870s that Stowe wrote *Palmetto Leaves*, a series of stories and sketches of Florida life, and entertained like-minded visitors from the North. Although the modest Stowe family cottage no longer stands, a commemorative marker is located at the Mandarin Community Club in the historic Harriet Beecher Stowe schoolhouse at 12447 Mandarin Drive. From I-95, take Exit 337 to merge onto I-295 N toward Orange Park. Take Exit #5B to merge onto San Jose Boulevard/SR-13. Turn right at Loretto Road, then left at Mandarin Road. The Community Club is located at the northern intersection of Mandarin and Brady roads.

OLD FORT LAUDERDALE VILLAGE AND MUSEUM (Broward County)

Known historically as the New River Inn, the Old Fort Lauderdale Village and Museum shares the history of the early peoples and pioneers of Broward County and Fort Lauderdale. The site, on the Broward Urban River Trail, features several preserved early 1900s homes and buildings located on the New River. Within the Village, the Inn is now a museum, and The Hoch Heritage Center houses a public research library and the area's largest historical collection of artifacts and photographs. The Fort Lauderdale Historical Society offers lectures, reenactments, and guided tours of the historic district and museum at 231 SW 2nd Avenue. From I-95, take the Broward Boulevard Exit and drive east on Broward Boulevard to Avenue of the Arts/SW 7th Avenue. Turn right on Avenue of the Arts/SW 7th Avenue to Himmarshee Street/SW 2nd Street. Turn left on Himmarshee Street/SW 2nd Street to SW 2nd Avenue, then turn right on SW 2nd Avenue.

ST. GEORGE EPISCOPAL CHURCH
(Duval County)

Built following the Reconstruction, the Carpenter Gothic-style church is located on Ft. George Island, which is one of several islands within Talbot Island State Park and the location of Florida's oldest plantation house (the home of Zephaniah and Anna Kingsley). Originally accessible only by boat, Ft. George Island gained popularity during the 1880s among tourists from the north. The church was added to the National Register of Historic Places in 2002 and remains an active parish today. From I-95 north of Jacksonville, take Exit 337 toward Jacksonville Beaches. Merge onto SR-9A N. Follow for about 20 miles and take the SR-105/Heckscher Drive exit toward Zoo Pkwy. Keep right at the fork, follow signs for Blount Island, and merge onto Heckscher Drive/SR-105 E. Continue to follow Heckscher Drive for 9.5 miles and bear left at Fort George Road.

CUBA AND FLORIDA

Native Americans in Florida and Cuba knew each other and had primitive trade long before the Spanish conquest and colonization. Cuban Natives called the island 90 miles from Key West by the name Cubanacan.

When we speak of "Cubans" in modern times, we are not speaking of the Native Cubans. Three Indian groups existed in Cubanacan when Columbus arrived in 1492 to discover, not America, but the Americas; specifically, he discovered Cuba, Hispaniola, and Puerto Rico. Even in Ponce de Leon's time, the Spanish thought Florida was a large island to the north, like Cuba.

Present-day Cubans are largely of Spanish decent. Perhaps 1,000 of the Native Cubans remain in Oriente Province. Although the Natives welcomed Columbus, the period of goodwill was short. The Spanish came not to assimilate, but to take over. They wanted gold, and failing in that, enslaved Native Americans to work their land. Native peoples were treated harshly. Most died outright from overwork and disease. Only a few survived to assimilate.

Florida, of course, was ruled from Havana during the lengthy period as a Spanish colony. That situation changed in 1821 after the transfer of flags.

During the Ten Year's War (1868-1878), a conflict between Cubans and Spain, many Cubans left the island. A large contingent of Cubans came to Key West, establishing a large Cigar making industry in that city. In 1886, prompted by labor unrest, better transportation, and favorable terms offered by Tampa's Board of Trade, manufacturer Vincente Martinez Ybor established his cigar-making operation in West Tampa, leading to the formation of Ybor City; its emergence as a vibrant industrial center containing immigrants from Cuba, Spain, Italy, and Germany dates from this period. On numerous occasions, the community hosted Cuban nationalist Jose Marti' and others, and Ybor City played a major role in bankrolling the movement for Cuban independence beginning in earnest in 1895.

When the U.S. battleship *Maine* blew up in Havana, the U.S. was quick to blame Spain. Jose Marti had rallied Florida for support of the Cuban independence movement. The U.S. used the sinking of the vessel as a pretext to invade Cuba, and the U.S. won a decisive victory. U.S. forces turned Cuba over to the Cubans. Cuban Independence Day is May 20, 1902, and is celebrated as *el Veinte de Mayo*.

Democracy in Cuba ended in 1952 when General Fulgencio Batista led a coup that toppled the elected government of President Carlos Prio. Opposing the ensuing dictatorship were guerilla forces led by Fidel Castro, his brother Raul, and a South American, named Che Guevera. Initially, Commandante Castro's forces were widely supported within the U.S. Shortly after the successful Cuban Revolution (1959), however, Castro's communist convictions became evident. President Kennedy's administration failed in its 1961 effort to invade Cuba with a debacle at the Bay of Pigs. Shortly thereafter, the world faced the threat of nuclear war when the Soviet Union attempted to place nuclear-armed missiles in Cuba. The Cuban Missile Crisis of 1962 ended peacefully when Nikita Khrushchev ordered missiles removed and missile launching facilities closed and construction halted; in return, American missiles were removed from Turkey.

Perhaps a million Cubanos have fled Cuba since the revolution. The largest concentrations of Cubans now live in Miami and Tampa.

As of this writing, Fidel Castro is still alive, although his brother, Raul, is now at the helm of state. Since early in his rule, when Fidel Castro identified himself as a communist, antagonism has existed between the U.S. and Cuba, including trade embargos hurtful to the Cuban people. A large population of anti-Castro Cuban exiles in the U.S. has influenced a hard-line approach to reconciliation between Cuban and the U.S. A new history will be written in the future, perhaps, one less antagonistic and with more democracy for Cuba.

➤ *Loading cannons onto a transport ship at Port Tampa during the Spanish–American War.*

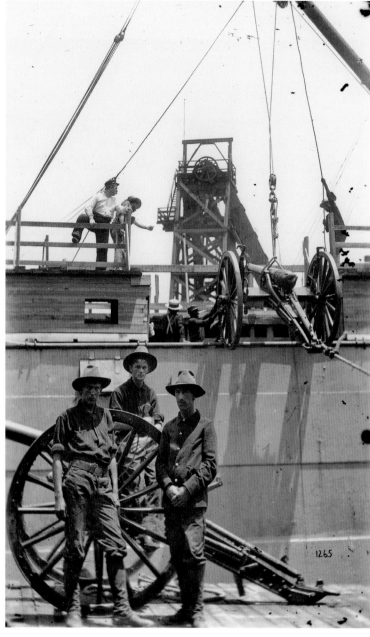

➤ *Cuban patriot, Jose Marti.*

⋏ *Troop ship loading from Port Tampa for the journey to Cuba during the Spanish–American War.*

33

⋏ Inside an Ybor City cigar factory. A lector, or reader, reads stories to entertain the workers.

Commercial cigar rolling first came to Florida in the 1830s and in the decades after the Civil War it became one of the most important industries in the southeastern United States. Cigar rolling grew from small-scale operations started by Cuban immigrants to encompass large, factory operations that attracted immigrants from throughout Europe and Latin America to Florida's growing cities.

There was a strong natural link between the cigar workers in Key West and Havana, and by the early 1890s, 50,000-100,000 people traveled back and forth annually.

Cigar manufacturing took place in all of Florida's urban areas at some point during the first century of statehood, but its impacts were particularly profound in Key West and in the Ybor City and West Tampa areas around Tampa Bay.

Although the industry declined from its height in the first decades of the 20th century after years of conflict between organized labor and factory management, the economic changes brought on by World War II, as well as mechanization of production and changing consumer demand for cigars, the legacy and cultural impact of the cigar industry and its workers remains a vibrant part of modern Florida.

➤ Cigar lady.

∧ *An aerial view of Fort Jefferson.*

DRY TORTUGAS NATIONAL PARK (Monroe County)

Construction on Fort Jefferson began in 1847 before the Civil War. Fort Jefferson, built at Garden Key, is allegedly the largest brick structure in the world, and was intended to counter Spanish influence at sea. Also, it protected an existing lighthouse and one built later at Loggerhead Key. The fortification saw extensive action during the Civil War and at times was used as a prison. Its most famous inmate was Dr. Samuel Mudd, jailed as a result of his part in the Lincoln assassination. Known as the "Gibraltar of the Gulf," Fort Jefferson is today part of Dry Tortugas National Park, 69 miles west of Key West and accessible only by boat. Construction of the fort was never completed because weapons improved to the point where it served little purpose. While there was frequent gunnery practice, no shots were ever fired in anger, unless it was the traditional anger of subordinates to superiors.

➢ *Old map shows location of Dry Tortugas.*

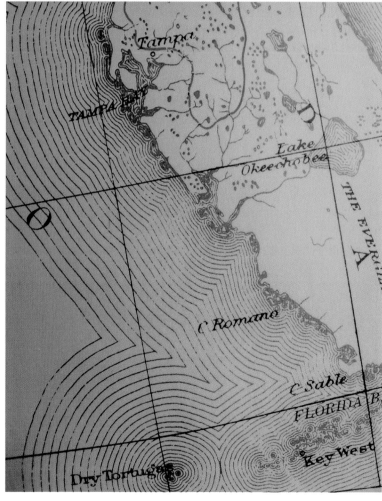

∧ *This brick road on Egmont Key once connected the fortifications, administrative areas, and barracks.*

EGMONT KEY (Hillsborough County)

What in the world, you might ask, is Egmont Key doing in Hillsborough County. After all, it lies in the mouth of Tampa Bay between Pinellas and Manatee counties. Blame it on the mapmakers, because half the mouth of the Bay (and a hearty part of it 7 miles from the mainland) is part of Hillsborough County. Egmont is a wonderful place to visit, although it can only be accessed by watercraft. There are pristine beaches, on which one might find relics (do not take artifacts), like ancient bullets, and fortifications from which shots were never fired in anger. A brick road remains, on which soldiers once marched and drilled. Gopher tortoises and Florida box turtles are plentiful on the island; and so are the swimmers and sunbathers under the watchful presence of a lighthouse. While some historians believe Ponce de Leon landed at the island, this has not been proven. Certainly Hernando de Soto passed by and may have landed on the island. Seminoles on the Trail of Tears were once briefly encamped on the island. Egmont's lighthouse was damaged by Confederate troops and its lens carted off. Union forces reclaimed the island shortly thereafter but not the lens. The first soldiers stationed permanently on the island arrived with the Civil War and lasted through the Spanish-American War. For the boat deprived, party boats from Manatee County bring visitors to the island. For a while, a hovercraft service went to the island both from the Pier in St. Petersburg and from Fort Desoto Park. It is possible to kayak from Fort Desoto at the southern tip of Pinellas County; however, there are stretches of rough water, even on calm days, and significant boating in the area. For a while at the end of the 1800s and into the early 1900s, Egmont was home to a military fort with hundreds of men, barracks, mess halls, and even a movie theater and bowling alley. Remnant brick roads can be walked where these buildings once stood.

FLORIDA CUBAN HERITAGE TRAIL
(Statewide)

This state-established trail, while including sites across many Florida counties, has the greatest number of historical sites in Key West, Dade County, and Tampa. A booklet delineating the more than 100 sites and including directions is available for a small fee from Florida Department of State, Division of Historical Resources (see Appendix A).

WORDS AND GERMS IN OLD YBOR

The tradition of the lector reading to the cigar workers as they labored is the subject matter of an award-winning play, *Anna and the Tropics*. Written by Nilo Cruz, the play describes the reactions of a family of cigar workers when a new lector reads from the Tolstoy novel, *Anna Karenina*. Lectors undoubtedly brightened the drudgery of cutting and wrapping fine Cuban tobacco and provided a sort of cultural education for the cigar workers.

In the fall of 1918, when the Great Spanish Influenza struck the Sunshine State, the close proximity of the cigar workers in the factories is thought to have helped spread the disease in Tampa. More than 20,000 residents of Hillsborough County were laid low by the virus; 4,000 Floridians died. However, blaming the cigar workers could be misplaced. Troops returning from World War I and Europe probably were the carriers of Spanish Flu to America. Read *One of Our Own* by Willa Cather.

FORT ZACHARY TAYLOR HISTORIC STATE PARK (Monroe County)

Fort Zachary Taylor is located near the southern tip of Key West. In addition to the fort, the 56-acre state park includes a public beach, bathhouse facilities, showers, a picnic area, and a nature trail. The construction of "Fort Zach," as the locals call it, was begun in 1845 and completed in 1866. In 1861, the fort was seized and held by Union forces, preventing the Confederacy from occupying Key West and discouraging Confederate blockade runners. Although it never saw action, the fort played an important strategic role in the Spanish-American War as well. It was remodeled in 1889 and outfitted with new ordnance. The old, outmoded cannons were buried on the grounds, along with their ammunition. As a result, Fort Zachary Taylor boasts the largest collection of Civil War era artillery in the U.S. Volunteers began the formidable task of unearthing the old guns in 1968 for restoration and display within the fort. The fort was included on the National Register of Historic Places in 1971 and received its National Historic Landmark designation in 1973. It opened to the public as a state park in 1985.

YBOR HISTORIC DISTRICT

(Hillsborough County)

Encouraged by ideal weather and improved railways, Martínez Ybor and Ignacio Haya relocated their Key West cigar factories to Tampa in the late 1800s. Manufacturers from Cuba and New York followed. Rapidly, 40 acres of Florida wilderness flourished into the "Cigar Capital of the World," producing up to 700 million hand-rolled cigars annually. However, automation in cigar manufacturing, a growing preference for cigarettes, and world war crushed the cigar industry. President Kennedy's 1962 Cuban Embargo effectively dowsed any remaining embers. For nearly three decades, poverty and slumlords ruled Ybor City. A smaller, Historic Ybor emerged in the 1990s. Grand structures and statues found throughout pay tribute to the vibrant tobacco trade. Today, pizza joints, pubs, tattoo parlors, and annual parades entertain the weekend crowds, while multi-screen movie complexes, upscale stores, and fine eateries entice the chic. Historic Ybor, located in the only portion of Tampa with sequentially numbered streets, is an easy exit from I-4 in Tampa. Secured public parking is available on 5th Avenue and 15th Streets. While strolling around Ybor City sipping *café con leche*, read the historic markers, and visit Ybor City Museum State Park, located at 1818 East 9th Avenue. They tell wonderful stories of cigars, revolution, the boom of an industry, and larger than life figures.

⋏ *Fort Zachery Taylor, current era.*

⋏ *A trolley car connects all of Ybor City to downtown Tampa.*

⋏ *Flagler's train crossing a bridge of the Overseas Railroad in the Florida Keys.*

Before highways and automobiles, before trucklines and buslines, railroads were the best method for moving goods about the state. Where railroads went, commerce followed. In many cases, modern roads follow old railroad beds, like US-1 going down the Keys. Passenger traffic by trains, while often romantic in concept, was probably very trying in its first days, but it sure beat the alternatives.

BAHIA HONDA STATE PARK
(Monroe County)

The rusting remains of Henry Flagler's railroad are best viewed from Bahia Honda State Park, 36850 Overseas Highway, 12 miles south of Marathon on US-1. The park's entrance is on the ocean side. Visitors can take a footpath from the main parking lot that leads to the northern bridge abutment, which is separate from the body of the bridge and has been converted to a fishing pier. This section of Flagler's railway bridge can also be viewed from the tip of Spanish Harbor Key, located just to the south, across the Bahia Honda Channel. Bahia Honda also sports perhaps the best natural beach in the Keys.

➢ *The beach at Bahia Honda.*

CEDAR KEY HISTORICAL MUSEUM
(Levy County)

Cedar Key has a long history, with Timucuan-speaking Native Americans believed to have lived on the islands in Cedar Keys as long ago as 2,500 years ago. Early military settlements proved tenuous, but after the Civil War, David Yulee built the railroad from Fernandina to Cedar Key, an event that caused a lumbering boom in (yes) cedar. Various industries have thrived and failed in Cedar Key, but fishing has always been a way of life. The railroad was 155.5 miles in length and used 5-foot gauge and 58-pound rail. The Florida Railroad was completed in March 1861 after 6 years of construction. From US-19 north of Crystal River and south of Chiefland, turn west on SR-24 and take it to the end. It is impossible to get lost in Cedar Key and the museum is easy to find. A nature trail along SR-24 approximately .5 miles north of the museum leads to a section of the original railroad. The town is Cedar Key, but the area with all the wonderful islands in it is called Cedar Keys. In common use, the two names are often interchangeable.

FLORIDA GULF COAST RAILROAD MUSEUM (Manatee County)

Several turn-of-the-century houses portend the museum's entrance as one discovers the museum and its connection to Florida railroad history. In 1911, this line became an addition to the Florida railroad system named "the Manatee Route." As diverse as the railroads lines that once crisscrossed Florida during the great railroad age, this collection of cars has been amassed from all over the country for display at the museum. The centerpiece is a 1916 Porter tank engine from the Brooklyn Naval Yards. Lining the tracks behind the quaint Parrish Depot are eleven cars, including three Pullman passenger cars, a Gondola Car, a "ticket Caboose," and a "Kentucky Club Car," converted in 1954 from a 1916 Pullman car. Visitors can enjoy a half-hour rural trip from Parrish that captures the feel of railroad travel back in the 1950s. When the train reaches Willow it reverses itself and ends back in Parrish. The Museum is 35 miles south of Tampa off I-75 at Exit 229 going east. Turn north on US-301 and the museum will shortly appear.

FLORIDA'S FIRST ATLANTIC TO GULF RAILROAD (Nassau County)

An historic marker at Atlantic Avenue and Front Street on Fernandina Beach memorializes the first cross-state railroad. It was launched by David Yulee in January 8, 1853 and was completed to Cedar Key on March 1, 1861 – just in time for the Civil War.

SEVEN-MILE BRIDGE (Monroe County)

The Seven-Mile Bridge begins just south of Marathon in the Keys, linking Knight's Key to Little Duck Key. Geographically, it marks the division between the middle and lower keys. The operating bridge parallels an earlier bridge constructed by Henry Flagler as part of his Overseas Railroad. The Seven-Mile Bridge passes the little island of Pigeon Key at Mosher Channel, about 1.5 miles from the bridge's northern terminus. Flagler built a camp there to house workers when the railway was constructed in 1909 to 1912. The Pigeon Key Foundation, located in a converted railroad car at Mile Marker 48 on Knight's Key, offers daily shuttle tours to the island on a replica locomotive dubbed the "Henry Express." Seven-Mile Bridge is actually a little short of that distance, perhaps 6.75 miles.

⋎ The old Seven-Mile Bridge in the Florida Keys.

Early Native Americans living in the Keys conducted minor trade with Native Americans to the south in Cuba and to the north along both Florida coasts. This early trade was conducted with relatively primitive dugout canoes and paddles and hardly qualifies as maritme trade of any significance.

By today's standards, the European explorers came in primitive craft, but these great boats were capable of carrying men and supplies around the world (albeit under harsh conditions). Storms and reefs claimed a large number of sailing craft, especially Spanish galleons as Spain began to colonize Florida. For the Spanish, safe passage was a priority for trade and hanging onto colonial possessions.

By the time the United States was a country, lighthouses were planned or built about Florida to prevent shipping accidents and promote shipping. The value of trade increased for the new country, and safe shipping lanes were an issue of national prosperity. Moreover, defending U.S. shores made safe shipping lanes a matter of national security.

Florida has a lot of coastline, over 1,500 miles. Shipping of goods by sea was (and is) a big-time business.

An independent industry had sprung up in the Keys because of all the wrecks. The Keys were famous for their "Wreckers" and "Salvers," and salvaging became a regulated industry in the newly established U.S. Perhaps the most dangerous Southern waters for shipping lie about the reefs and shoals along the Keys and to the west of the Keys.

Lighthouses constructed there were so vulnerable to storms that a new kind of design was needed, the so-called "screw-pile" lighthouses, with structures screwed into the coral rock. Lighthouses were so important for safe conduct of U.S. trade that upon the founding of the U.S., selection of lighthouse was overseen by no less than George Washington, the "father of the country." Nowadays the lighthouses and other maritime aids to navigation are the province of the U.S. Coast Guard. Not many lights are manned any longer and most are automatically operated.

How many lighthouses have been or are in Florida is a matter of debate. Purists believe that lighthouses must have had a keeper and keeper's quarters, but many lighthouses have been designed to operate with a minimum of aid, and no lighthouses have anyone living there to operate them on a daily basis any longer.

Amazingly, Tierra Verde Lighthouse joined the list of Florida lighthouses in the 21st century and sits atop the education and administration building of Tampa Bay Watch on Tierra Verde in Pinellas County.

Today luxury cruise ships set out from Miami, Tampa, and other ports to Mexico and tropical islands, but those Florida ports are also major shipping centers for an enormous quantity of goods going to and coming from around the world. Billions of dollars in annual trade flow through a variety of ports in Florida, but the largest state port in terms of tonnage is that of Port Tampa. By tonnage, Tampa is the 16th largest port in the U.S. Moreover, Tampa is a global port.

Other Florida ports include Penasocola, Panama City, Port Manatee, Fernandina, Jacksonville, Canaveral, Fort Pierce, Port of Miami-Dade, Port Everglades, Port of Key West, and others. (Ohr for all accounts within this section)

APALACHICOLA MARITIME MUSEUM
(Franklin County)

There was an active port in the area in the early 1800s supporting the cotton trade. During the Civil War, the port was blockaded and retaken by Union forces. The Apalachicola River originates now at Lake Seminole, but in the early days was directly connected to the Chattahootchee River. Freshwater travels over 100 miles to create the estuary at the river mouth. Oyster harvesting and sports fishing are present-day industries in "Apalach" and the surrounding areas. The museum engages in boat building, education, paddling trips on the river and in the area, sailing trips (some far and wide), and noble restoration work. When going west over the bridge across Apalachicola Bay, look to the north to see the rich estuary and to the south to view the Gulf of Mexico. After descending from the bridge, make a right from US-98 onto Avenue C, proceed a few blocks to the waters edge and Water Street. The museum address is 103 Water Street. Apalachicola is an old Florida town steeped in history, with old homes, a graveyard, old churches, and a museum dedicated to John Gorrie, who cooled yellow fever patients with ice and created the concept for modern air-conditioning.

CAPE FLORIDA LIGHTHOUSE (Dade County)

The original lighthouse built at this location was burned to the ground by Seminoles in 1836. In the process, the lighthouse keeper was severely injured and burned and his assistant, probably a slave, was killed. The current lighthouse has survived the Civil War and numerous hurricanes, including a direct hit from Hurricane Andrew, a Category-5 storm, in 1992. Placed on the National Register of Historic Places in 1971, Cape Florida Lighthouse is located in Bill Baggs Cape Florida State Park, which attracts nearly a million visitors a year – not all for the lighthouse, for the beaches are wonders. South of Miami on US-1, turn east on Rickenbacker Causeway. The causeway is continued by Crandon Boulevard which leads to the park.

JUPITER INLET LIGHTHOUSE
(Palm Beach County)

General George Meade defeated General Robert E. Lee at Gettysburg, in effect ending the Civil War. Long before Meade was victoriously defending the nation, he was a lighthouse engineer. He designed several lighthouses in Florida, including the one at Jupiter Inlet. Like many lighthouses in Florida, it was put out of action by Confederate forces during the Civil War. At 108-feet tall and with a red daymark, the lighthouse stands out in the flat land at the edge of the Atlantic Ocean. The lighthouse was placed on the National Register of Historic Places in 1973. With the exception of the Civil War, the lighthouse has operated since 1860. Go east on Indian Gap Road from I-95 to US-1. Go north on US-1. The lighthouse will appear in approximately 2 miles.

KEY WEST LIGHTHOUSE (Monroe County)

The original lighthouse, built in 1825, was destroyed in a storm in 1846 with the death of 14, devastating the keeper's family. The same hurricane took down the Sand Key Lighthouse across the channel with the death of six, including that keeper. The replacement lighthouse at Key West went into service in 1847 and operated until it was de-activated in 1969, a span of 122 years. In 1972, the lighthouse was leased to the Key West Art and Historical Society and became a private aid to navigation. It is now on the National Register of Historic Places. It is impossible to miss the lighthouse once on the island of Key West. Not only is the lighthouse an excellent spot to visit, but it is in close proximity to a number of other historic locations worthy of visit, including Hemingway's House and Truman's Little White House, among others. The museum at the lighthouse is excellent and a giant Fresnel lens is on display. A Frenel lens was a work of art, a means of intensifying light. The Key West Lighthouse also had an independent lady keeper who lost her children in that Great Hurricane of 1846.

MARITIME HERITAGE TRAIL/ BISCAYNE NATIONAL PARK (Dade County)

The National Park Service is creating its only underwater trail, soon to be open to the public. Five of the wrecks on the trail can be visited with scuba gear, while one (a schooner) can be visited with the aid of snorkels. All require boats to reach. The wrecks range from 1878 to 1966. At the time of its sinking (1913), *The Lugano* was the largest vessel ever go down in the Keys. The wreck of *The Alicia* was a potential bonanza for key wreckers and salvers, with over 70 competing groups trying to get the valuable goods; maritme law was rewritten after this wreck. Biscayne National park is in Homestead.

⋏ *Key West Lighthouse.*

PANAMA CANAL MUSEUM (Pinellas County)

In modern times, the Panama Canal is taken for granted. Before its existence, however, ships had to sail round the southern tip of South America to enter the Pacific. The 48-mile canal saved thousands of miles at sea. Moreover, a passage around Cape Horn was exceptionally dangerous. The first European to "discover" the Pacific was Vasco Nunez de Balboa, a man who was busy conquering Native Americans in the area when a local leader mentioned the "new" sea. Balboa was a Spainard, and Charles V, King of Spain, saw the possibility of a canal as long as four and half centuries ago. The first attempt to build the canal took place by the French in the 1880s and resulted in almost 22,000 deaths largely due to malaria and yellow fever. Americans took a large number of fatalities too when they took up the job in the 1900s. Approximately 5,600 more human lives were lost under the American effort. The dreaded tropical diseases were contained through the efforts of Dr. William Gorgas and his "mosquito brigade" of nurses and West Indian laborers. The Panama Canal, which opened to world commerce on August 15, 1914, made the global economy possible.

The Panama Canal Museum contains photographs, artifacts, and memoriabilia from the construction and operation periods. One might well ask how did a Panama Canal Museum come to be established in Seminole. The answer is that there have always been close ties between the canal and Florida. The theme of the 1910 Gasparilla Festival celebrated the Panama Canal construction. Generations of Americans retiring from the Panama Canal Company relocated in Pinellas to be close to family and friends still in the Canal Zone. With the prospect of the canal being turned over to Panama on December 31, 1999, former employees (concerned about losing the heritage of their beloved Canal Zone) founded the museum to preserve this unique history of the U.S. in Panama.

From I-275 between St. Petersburg and Largo, take exit 28 toward Pinellas Park/Seminole on SR-694 West (Park Boulevard), then turn north on 113th Street. The address and website are in appendix A.

A *Fresnel lens was an important part of the equipment at many early lighthouses. It focused the light from the lamp and greatly improved the range of the light. Many Fresnel lens could be considered works of art.*

PONCE DE LEON INLET LIGHTHOUSE
(Volusia County)

This impressive lighthouse is constructed of more than 250,000 red bricks. At its base, the bricks are 8 feet thick. The second lighthouse built in the area, it has an impressive focal plane of 159 feet. "Focal plane" is the height of the lighthouse's light above mean sea level. Building the lighthouse in the 1880s was no easy task; historians record the loss of at least a dozen lives in a then remote area known as Mosquitoe Inlet. Talk about hardship: imagine the task of toting oil for the lamps up 213 steps to the lattern room. High school English classes have undoubtedly made the Mosquitoe Inlet Lighthouse well known, for it is the lighthouse glimpsed in the distance in Stephen Crane's immortal short story, "The Open Boat." The light-house was declared a National Historic Landmark by the Secretary of the Interior in 1998. It was earlier (1972) placed on the National Register of Historic Places. The lighthouse is part of an operating light station and has an excellent museum. From the northern end of I-4, go south on I-95 to the Dunlawton Avenue exit. Go 5 miles south to the light station.

◁ *Ponce de Leon Inlet Lighthouse is a favorite visit for tourists and residents alike.*

⋏ *Port Boca Grand Lighthouse.*

PORT BOCA GRAND LIGHTHOUSES
(Charlotte and Lee counties)

Although the cattle trade with Cuba had something to do with it, Port Boca Grande became active with the boom in the phosphate industry in the 1880s. A railroad was built to the port, primarily to carry phosphate. Port Boca Grande Lighthouse is in a wooden structure that is very houselike and serves as the home for a museum and gift shop. The lighthouse was supplemented by the Boca Grande Rear-Range Light. The two lights cast beacons that crossed. Mariners entering the harbor could avoid the shoals if they kept the lights aligned. The rear-range light looks more like what most of us think of as a lighthouse. There is a great deal of largely mythical pirate folklore in the area. The site is managed by Gasparilla Island State Park. Among the joys of visiting are beach walks and plunges

into the surf. The island is also home to a population of iguanas descended from escaped pets; if exterminating plans have failed, as they probably will, the visitor can still find plenty of reptile company to enjoy. South of Sarasota, exit I-75 on River Road and cross US-41. The road then becomes CR-775. After a few miles, take a turn onto CR-771, which has a toll bridge to Gasparilla Island on which the lighthouses are located. The signs will take the visitor to the lighthouse and museum, while the rear-range light will become evident.

SS AMERICAN VICTORY MARINERS MEMORIAL AND MUSEUM SHOP
(Hillsborough County)

Anchor your place in American Maritime History by coming aboard a fully functioning, 1940s era steamship. This maritime icon served in WWII and during

the Korean and Vietnam wars. Experience an unforgettable voyage of discovery by exploring a restored ship of a bygone era. Brought to Tampa in 1999, the American Victory Ship now serves as a mariner's memorial and museum. Relive history and visit cavernous, three-level cargo holds, a radio room, hospital, gallery, weaponry, mess hall, engine room, and crew cabins, as well as see photographs, medals, documents, and more. The American Victory Ship is located directly behind the Florida Aquarium in the Channelside District of downtown Tampa. For Channelside, take the downtown exit of I-275 in the heart of Tampa and follow the Channelside signs. Once in the area, the visitor will want to be sure to go to the nearby Tampa Aquarium.

DREAMERS, EXPLORERS, IDEALISTS, INDUSTRIALISTS, AND POWER BROKERS

It started with the Spanish and has not stopped since; visionaries coming to Florida to make a fortune or to make the world better (or at least in their image). It is fair to say that few areas of the U.S. have attracted so many dreamers, industrialists, idealists, explorers, and power brokers.

ALFRED B. MACLAY GARDENS STATE PARK (Leon County)

The very best time to visit Maclay Gardens is during the week, maybe on a day with a little drizzle, so one can have it alone and undisturbed. Wander among thousands of plants in the quietude of a retreat near the busy heart of the city of Tallahassee. The gardens were originally a hobby for Alfred Maclay, who first planted them at his newly purchased winter home. He named them Killearn Gardens for the place in Scotland where his family originated. After his passing, his family gave the gardens to the state. Among the highlights are the tour of the historical house, a reflecting pool, a hidden garden, and a walled garden. Lake Hall and Lake Overstreet are within the state park; the Overstreet section was added in a later acquisition. There is a 3.5-mile lake trail that is beloved by joggers and walkers. From I-10 in Tallahassee, take the Thomasville Road exit north. Brown signs announce the westward turn into the road leading to the gardens.

ARCHBOLD BIOLOGICAL STATION

(Highlands County)

Archbold Biological Station is named for explorer, scientist, and aviator Richard Archbold (1907-1976). In the 1920s and 1930s, Richard Archbold explored faraway corners of the earth most of us will never get to visit. These included such exotic locations as Madagascar and Papua, New Guinea. The world was not quite as well known then. People had a better idea what was on the moon than on some of the more remote locations of the world. Movies could display giant apes found on warm tropical islands (*King Kong*) or posit exotic creatures living at the South Pole (H. P. Lovecraft's novel *At the Mountains of Madness*). Of course, Archbold was not looking for giant apes or monster-dominated cities from antiquity, nor could they be found, but the zoological and botanical wonders encountered on these expeditions furthered scientific knowledge from some of the more remote areas of the world. These were not easy expeditions 80 or more

years ago. Archbold went to rugged places and encountered hardships. When World War II brought Archbold's explorations to a halt, he intended a short interruption in his explorations, but the war dragged on for five long years. During that time, Archbold stayed at the present location of the station and developed a great interest in the area. In the 1930s, the buildings at Archbold Biological Station were built by Alexander Blair for Donald Roebling II, the son of the man who built the Brooklyn Bridge. John was an inventor in his own right, a maverick and cantankerous engineer who built "Roebling's alligator," a prototype amphibious assault vehicle donated to the War Department, and used in the Pacific Theater (see accounts in the section on World War II). Roebling graciously donated the property to Archbold Expeditions. The research station is not open to just visit, although they certainly will not turn you away. Rather it is open by appointment for tours. A tour should be taken for many reasons. First, in 2007 the station went on The National Register of Historic Places for its architecture, scientific research, and contribution to conservation. Moreover, the station sits in a scrub environment on part of the Lake Wales Ridge. Thanks to funding from Archbold Expeditions, the station is a preeminent research facility and a source of knowledge that this author has drawn on many times.

Archbold Biological Station is located off SR-70. This state road has a west exit on I-95 near Fort Pierce and an east exit on I-75 near Bradenton. The station is roughly in-between. To the west of US-27 in Lake Placid, take a southerly turn on Old State Road 6. The station will appear shortly on the west side of the road. Historical tours and tour of the valuable scrub habitat can be arranged by calling ahead. A learning center is underway for the future, but it is not forecast to be complete for several years.

BARNACLE HISTORIC STATE PARK

(Dade County)

Webster's describes a barnacle as a small marine crustacean that attaches itself tenaciously to rocks and ships. There was a South Florida pioneer who, in much the same way, tenaciously attached himself to this part of Florida and named his home, "The Barnacle"-- Ralph Middleton Munroe. Today the Barnacle is the oldest house in Dade County still standing on its original site and is the centerpiece of

Barnacle Historic State Park. Munroe grew up on Staten Island and became enamored with boats at an early age. The story goes that in 1877, he traveled to Biscayne Bay by way of Key West. Key West was a deep-water port; Biscayne Bay is very shallow and could not accommodate the larger vessels. One had to go to Key West, then board smaller vessels that could hug the coast to return north to Biscayne Bay.

When Munroe's wife was diagnosed with tuberculosis, he brought her to Miami for a change of climate in hopes she would get better. They left their infant daughter with his mother in New York and camped on the banks of the Miami River in winter. Sadly, his wife Eva succumbed to her disease. Upon returning to New York, Munroe learned of his daughter's death from influenza. Several times afterward, Munroe returned to Biscayne Bay, but he did not purchase land until 1886. It wasn't until then that he began making his home in Coconut Grove. Munroe lived in his boathouse on the water before completing The Barnacle in 1891. It has the dubious distinction of having the first floor of the house built after the second floor. It seems when additional space was needed he simply jacked the first floor up and built the second floor beneath.

In time, Munroe became a boat builder, activist, pioneer photographer, and salvager of wrecked ships. Munroe met Miss Jessie Wirth on a cruise in 1894 and married for the second time. As a leader in the Coconut Grove community he fought the good fight thwarting attempts by developers to build artificial reefs offshore and pump raw sewage into the Bay. Munroe died in 1933 leaving his hammock grove a vestige of what Miami must have looked like before the turn-of-the-century.

From US-1, proceed east on SW 27th Avenue. Turn right on South Bayshore Drive; it becomes McFarlane. Continue to Main Highway Intersection and take a sharp left on Main Highway.

BOK TOWER GARDENS (Polk County)

During the last global epoch, the land where Bok Tower and its famous gardens is located was an island in a sea that covered much of Florida. Today a 205-foot tall carillon tower with 60 bells stands atop the highest point (298 feet in elevation) in Lake Wales Ridge. To find higher land in Florida, one must travel to the Panhandle.

Edward William Bok was a Dutch immigrant; his family came to the U.S. in 1869 when he was six years old. Like many immigrants, he worked hard to pay for his education beyond the Brooklyn public school system. In 1882, he took a position with the publisher Henry Holt and Company. Two years later, he went to work for the publisher Scribner and Sons. Today Bok is best known for his tower and for editing *The Ladies Home Journal*. The magazine, under Bok's tutelage, became the first magazine in the world to achieve one-million subscribers. Bok was also the author of eleven books, and his autobiography (*The Americanization of Edward Bok*) won the Pulitzer Prize. His autobiography is available within the Gardens' incredible gift shop. Bok was a social activist and early environmentalist. He had pioneering ideas in sex education, neo-natal care, and childcare. He was also a pacifist and yearned for world peace. He established several charities and left the world The American Foundation, now known as The Bok Tower Gardens Foundation.

In a state where jet planes streak the air at all hours, and where interstate highways are always in use by tourists and residents, Bok Tower is perhaps the most peaceful refuge in Florida. Touring its gardens with seemingly endless rows of plants and sitting beneath the great tower listening to the soothing chimes is a cure for melancholy if there ever was one.

From I-4 east of Tamp, go south on US-27 for 23 miles. Turn east on Mountain Lake Cut Off Road, then south on CR-17/17A. In 1.3 miles, a sign indicates the direction to the Gardens. Signs lead the way.

⋏ *The ornate gold gateway to the tower.*

⋎ *The "Singing Tower" at Lake Wales, a 1951 postcard view.*

⅄ *A recent photo of The Breakers, the historic Palm Beach hotel built by Henry Flagler.*

THE BREAKERS (Palm Beach County)

The Breakers started its varied life as the Palm Beach Inn in 1896. Renamed The Breakers following a major renovation a few years later, the hotel was severally damaged by fire in 1903. Henry Flagler, an oil and Florida railroad tycoon, insisted on rebuilding. The Breakers reopened within a year. Another fire in 1925, however, destroyed the nearly all-wooden resort. The Flagler family refused defeat, promising a replacement far grander than its predecessor. The results of their determination are evident in the seven-story Italian Renaissance masterpiece that continues enticing the elite and awestruck to Florida's east coast. The Breakers was named to the National Register of Historic Places in 1973. From I-95, take the exit for Okeechobee Boulevard/SR-704E toward Downtown. Follow SR-704E to South Flagler Drive. Turn left onto South Flagler, then bear right back onto SR-704E/ Lakeview Avenue for about another mile. Turn left at South County Road. The hotel is on the right.

THE CASEMENTS (Volusia County)

The Casements was the winter home of Standard Oil billionaire, John D. Rockefeller, Sr. Named for its decorative Casement Windows, the house was purchased by Rockefeller in 1918, and he owned it until his death in 1937 at the age of 97. Rockefeller first wintered across the street in the famous Ormond Beach Hotel but allegedly got mad when he was charged more than the other guests. At that point, he purchased the house across the street built by Reverend Harwood Huntington for his wife in the early 1900s. Rockefeller thought the mild Florida winters might extend his longevity (perhaps he was right, as he did live to 97). Having arrived in Ormond Beach with 27 servants, Rockefeller made some changes to the property but they were not considered lavish. The Casement's tranquil setting overlooks the Halifax River with its terraced lawns sloping down beneath shade trees to the water. A partner with Henry Flagler in founding the Standard Oil Company, Rockefeller was reported at the time to be earning a cool $300,000 a day. Entertaining was a top priority at the Casements, where its rotunda saw such dignitaries as Will Rogers, Henry Ford, and Harvey Firestone. Christmas parties were a tradition at the Casements, where friends and neighbors gathered each year. The distinctive oil baron could be seen in town at the annual street fair dispensing mint dimes to kids, as was his custom. One of the dimes provided good luck during a 1927 Daytona Speed Race when Sir Malcolm Campbell was behind the wheel of his Bluebird Race Car. He topped out at 253 mph with a Rockefeller dime in his pocket. From 1941 until 1951, the Casements operated as an exclusive girl's school by Maude Van Woy, owner of the Fairmont Junior College of Washington, D.C. Changes at that time included the addition of a dormitory wing. The Casements was almost lost to vandals in the 1970s, but a fight to save it resulted in its placement upon the National Register of Historic Places, spurring a $500,000 grant in 1977. This marked the first phase of restoration in modern times. Today, the City of Ormond Beach owns the property and uses it for exercise, computer, music, and cooking classes. The Casement Guild (begun in 1979) serves as a volunteer organization that supports the historic property in part by operating a Gift Shop and providing informative daily tours. In Ormond Beach, go east on East Granada Boulevard, crossing the Halifax River. Turn right on Riverside Drive. The Casements is located at 25 Riverside Drive.

EDISON AND FORD WINTER HOMES (Lee County)

Thomas Alva Edison came to Fort Myers in 1885 looking for a better filament for his light bulbs. Instead, he got a wife, Mina Miller. Apparently it was a successful marriage, producing three children. Edison and Henry Ford first met when Ford was an employee of the Detroit Edison Illumination Company. By then, Ford had built prototype cars, including his Quadricycle (1896). Edison encouraged Ford, and the two men became friends over time. Ford purchased his home to spend the winters with his friend. Edison, a farm boy known to his father as Al, changed the world. Electric light, movies, and sound recordings owe their existence in large part to Edison. At 23, he sold his first invention, a universal stock ticker, for an astounding sum of $40,000. After that, he never looked back, but continued a stream of inventions and modifications that became the future. He recorded 1093 patents and at least one patent a year from 1868 to 1933. What most people don't know is that Edison was hearing impaired. He suffered from scarlet fever as a boy. He was totally deaf in one ear and only had 10% hearing in the other. He probably could hear a foghorn, if reasonably close, but not a whisper or normal speech, unless the speaker was next to Edison's good ear. Edison, however, did not see this as a handicap but as an asset. He had no time for small talk, he said, thus could focus his mind on his work. Ford's Model T, or "Tin Lizzie," certainly revolutionized the future also. Ford created mass production of the automobile and made autos affordable to the common man. Perhaps there are no two bigger giants of their time in industry. The City of Fort Myers was given Edison's Home by his wife, Mina, in 1947, and acquired the Ford Home in 1988. It includes a total of 9 historical buildings and 20 botanical gardens. Within the gardens are over 500 species of plants and trees. The Edison and Ford Homes are located along McGregor Drive just to the west of US-41 in Fort Myers. They are on the south side of Caloosahatchee River. US-41 can be reached from any of the I-75 exits in Fort Myers. For reaching the Edison Home, the two northernmost exits will spare the driver from having to creep north on US-41.

FAIRCHILD TROPICAL BOTANICAL GARDENS (Dade County)

The life of David Fairchild (1869-1954) is one of great exploration. He was not quite Indiana Jones, but he was certainly wide-ranging in his pursuit of tropical plants that might be of benefit to his countrymen. He scoured the world, bringing Americans such things as alfalfa, bamboos, dates, flowering cherries, horseradish, nectarines, and soybeans among others. How he found time to marry the younger daughter of Alexander Graham Bell and father children is a good question, or how he had time to write so many scientific papers and four books, for he collected over 200,000 exotic plant species from around the world during the time of his explorations. Before he became such a renowned plant explorer, he supervised the Division of Plant Introduction in Washington, D.C. South Florida is blessed with semi-tropical to tropical weather capable of supporting plant life from those regions. In short, it stays warm, doesn't snow or freeze, and rains a lot. When Fairchild retired to Miami in the 1930s, he met and befriended Colonel Robert H. Montgomery, himself a plant enthusiast. Montgomery created (1938) the 83-acre Fairchild Tropical Botanical Gardens, naming it for his esteemed friend. On subsequent trips about the world, Fairchild collected and planted many of the living things that visitors can enjoy in present days. This includes the giant baobab tree near the entrance. Portions of the gardens complex are historical monuments. The gardens are located at 10901 Old Cutler Road in Coral Gables. Old Cutler Road is a coastal drive to the east of US-1.

⋏ *Thomas Edison, naturalist and author John Burroughs, and Henry Ford at Fort Myers.*

⋏ *Fairchild Gardens is known for its outstanding collection of tropical plants and trees.*

▲ *This photo illustrates why the Fakahatchee Strand is called the "Amazon of North America."*

FAKAHATCHEE STRAND BIOLOGICAL STATE PARK (Collier County)

"A strand swamp is a shallow, elongated channel within limestone plain dominated by bald cypress trees." (Ohr, *Florida's Fabulous Natural Places,* 1999) Nestled between Alligator Alley to the north, the Big Cypress, and Ten Thousand Islands to the south, the Fakahatchee Strand encompasses nearly 74,000 acres of wetland wilderness. Often called the "Amazon of North America," the Strand is a 20 by 5-mile swath of sloughs and lake swamps teaming with rare wildlife and cypress forest. Paleo-Indians (12,000 to 7,500 BC) frequented the area for its deep waterholes and abundant game. Modern man, plume hunters, and poachers earned profits from the semitropical flora and fauna. However, lumber mills and shyster developers of the mid-1940s coveted even more from the ecological wonder: the seemingly endless groves of virgin cypress forest. Cypress logging began in 1913. By World War II, the weekly harvest totaled nearly 1 million board feet. Extensive clear-cutting, drainage, and roadwork prompted land developers to purchase the area in the mid-1960s for a housing project. Ironically, the development company's (Gulf American Land Company—later known as GAC) illegal dredging and filling miles away saved the Strand from devastation. As retribution for their violations in Cape Coral, nearly 10,000 acres of the Strand were turned over to the state. The Fakahatchee Strand, now protected as an Endangered Land, entered the state park system two years later. Through ongoing preservation efforts the park has grown seven-fold to date and continues reclaiming its natural state. South of Naples from I-75 exit on SR-29 south and proceed to the community of Copeland where the Strand is a right hand (westerly) turn.

▼ *The rare and illusive ghost orchid is found in only a very few places other than the Fakahatchee Strand.*

◁ *A recent view of the Flagler Memorial Presbyterian Church built by Henry Flagler in 1890.*

FLAGLER MEMORIAL PRESBYTERIAN CHURCH (St. Johns County)

As Henry Flagler continued expanding his Florida Empire through southbound railroads and majestic hotels, tragedy struck. In 1889, his daughter, Jenny, died during childbirth while en route to St. Augustine. In memory of Jenny and her lost child, Flagler constructed the solid-poured, concrete, Venetian Renaissance-style church in 1890. With its hand-carved woodwork, towering copper-clad dome, and massive Greek cross, the stunning Flagler Memorial Church, at 32 Sevilla Street, is home to the oldest Presbyterian congregation in Florida. Open for free public tours, the church is the final resting-place for Henry Flagler, his first wife, and his beloved daughter. From I-95, Take Exit #318. Turn east on SR-16 to US-1 South (N. Ponce de Leon Boulevard). Turn (L) left at Carrera, go about two blocks, then turn right at Sevilla Street.

FRANK LLOYD WRIGHT VISITOR CENTER, FLORIDA SOUTHERN COLLEGE CAMPUS (Polk County)

Florida Southern College was founded in 1883 and is associated with the United Methodist Church. A private college, it offers 46 undergraduate degrees. Praised nationally for its academic program, it overlooks Lake Hollingsworth. The architecture of its campus stands in testimony to an architectural genius, Frank Lloyd Wright. Florida Southern has the largest collection of Wright's buildings in one location in the world, as well as guided tours of the work. The visitor is most likely to be impressed with the Annie Pfeiffer Chapel, constructed with student labor from 1939-1941. Within the Chapel, the wall lines seem to melt into one another. On top of the building stands wrought-iron work referred to as "the bowtie." Other buildings on the campus designed by Wright include the William H. Danforth Chapel, containing original pews and leaded glass, six other buildings, a pool and fountain complex, and covered walkways. From I-4 east of Tampa, exit south at exit 33. Proceed to Memorial Boulevard and turn east. Turn south on Ingraham Avenue and proceed to Lake Hollingsworth Avenue. The college is on the east side of the lake.

HARBOR OAKS HISTORIC DISTRICT (Pinellas County)

The Harbor Oaks Historic District was the first such district in Pinellas County when a historic marker was erected in 1988. Opened by Dean Alvord in 1914, Harbor Oaks was Clearwater's first planned subdivision. A major developer in New York State, Alvord brought forward-thinking planning techniques. Instead of merely platting out a bare sub-division on septic tank, Dean Alvord utilized sewers, sidewalks, paved streets, curbs, parkways, and street lighting. Harbor Oaks represented the early use of the deed restriction ensuring less commercial intrusion into residential areas and establishing a rich architectural mix of two and three-story dwellings. Alvord dubbed his new subdivision "the Riviera of the Sunny South" and "the finest shore development on the West Coast of Florida." Luring his wealthy New York friends to Clearwater to invest in Harbor Oaks resulted in an eclectic mix of architectural styles ranging from Mediterranean to Tudor to Colonial revival and bungalows. The neighborhood exuded the atmosphere of a wealthy pocket of the northeast and was reminiscent of places like Garden City, Long Island, where Alvord did a lot of early building. Harbor Oaks is a relatively small district and can be walked or driven quite easily. A good starting point is the freestanding historic marker on Bay Avenue in the middle of the neighborhood. The centerpiece of the district is the Magnolia Street Dock, site of sunset watching, weddings, picnics, fishing, or just socializing. Famous personages residing in Harbor at one time include: Donald Roebling, inventor of the WWII amphibious tank," the Alligator;" Charles Ebbets, owner of the Brooklyn Dodgers; Robert S. Brown, who patented the Ford Motor car paint in the 1920s; J.M. Studebaker, of the Studebaker automobile family; famous race car driver, Nigel Mansell; Robert Ingersol of Ingersol-Rand Company; Broadway choreographer, Ann Renkin; Phillies' shortstop Larry Bowa; and author, Rex Beach. Proceed south from central Clearwater on South Ft. Harrison Avenue to Druid Road. Turn right on Druid Road to the historic maker at Druid and Bay Avenue. From US-19, take SR-60 to South Fort Harrison

The Clearwater Sea-monster

Reports of sea-monsters abound worldwide and have taken root in Florida at times. In 1948, Clearwater Beach made national news when an innocent stroller in February came upon footprints of monstrous proportions and alerted local authorities. The creature appeared to have 6-foot strides and walked 2 miles of the beach. A noted zoologist, Ivan T. Sanderson, claimed to have investigated similar tracks on the Suwannee River, and promptly proclaimed a species known as "Florida three-toes." The monster was actually the invention of local resident Toni Signorini and his business partner, Al Williams. Signori fabricated the monster feet from cast iron in a foundry. From a rowboat, Signorini came ashore wearing the feet. By alternating between stepping in the surf and on the beach, he was able to leave footprints with such a great distance between them.

⅄ *An historic postcard view of the namesake palm thatch honeymoon cottages on Honeymoon Island.*

HONEYMOON ISLAND STATE PARK
(Pinellas County)

Clinton Moseley Washburn made national headlines in 1938 when he bought a remote barrier island off Dunedin for $25,000 and offered free honeymoons to youthful newlyweds from all over America. He re-named what the locals called Hog Island (after an failed hog venture on the island) and called it Honeymoon Island. He adorned the Gulf side with 50 quaint palm-thatch huts, a meeting hall, and just enough amenities to provide the honeymooners with a brief stay in "paradise." In 1964, a bridge and causeway connected the island to the mainland and an unsuccessful development project left the beach scattered with cement and block. The state wisely stepped in, purchased the land, restored it, and due to these worthy efforts, Honeymoon Island on the Gulf does look like paradise. There is an excellent trail system for the interior of the island and great swimming. From US-19 north of Clearwater and south of Tarpon Springs, turn west on SR-580 to SR-586, which leads into the park.

HENRY B. PLANT MUSEUM
(Hillsborough County)

While the two great railroad magnates, Henry Plant and Henry Flagler, were developing Florida, Plant sent Flagler an invitation to a huge hotel Plant had just built in Tampa in 1891. Flagler sent back a telegram asking, "Where's Tampa?" Plant shot back, "Just follow the crowds." Originally the Tampa Bay Hotel, Plant Museum sits on the campus of the University of Tampa, a private college. Famous New York architect J. A. Wood is responsible for the design, including adorning minarets. Mr. and Mrs. Plant visited Europe to bring back antiques, artwork, and lavish furnishings for the hotel described in 1891 by the *New York Times* as "one of the grandest hotels in the country." Plant died in 1899 at the age of 79, and the hotel was sold to the City of Tampa in 1905 at a fire-sale price—$125,000. Plant spent $3,000,000 building and furnishing the hotel. The University of Tampa bought the hotel in 1933. Plant Museum and the UT campus are located along Kennedy Boulevard just to the west of downtown Tampa. From I-275, take the Ashley Street exit south to Kennedy and turn west. Shortly, the minarets will come into view.

KORESHAN STATE HISTORIC SITE
(Lee County)

In 1894, Dr. Cyrus Teed, a New York physician, came to Florida intending to build a New Jerusalem for 10 million followers. His name ("Cyrus") in Hebrew is Koresh, and the religion he founded is called Koreshanity. Teed believed many strange things, among them that humans lived within a giant sphere instead of outside of one. He had become an alchemist during the Civil War. The Koreshan Community that Teed founded was on land owned by a Russian immigrant named Dam Kohler. Teed converted Kohler, who donated the land on which the site was built. Requirements to be a Koreshan included abstinence from sex, alcohol, or tobacco. The site, when thriving, contained a power plant, boathouse, bakery, general store, machine shops, observatory, an art center, community hall, trails, and gardens. Teed, who announced to his followers that he would return to life six days after death, disappointed them in 1908. The Koreshan Community deeded a reduced parcel of land to Florida in 1961. Lillian "Vesta" Newcomb believed in Teed her whole life, until she saw men walk on the moon and lost her belief in a hollow earth. From I-75 south of Ft. Myers, the Estero exit is clearly marked and leads west to US-41. The site is straight across US-41 on the northwest corner.

⅄ *One of the old buildings at Koreshan State Historic Site.*

MARIE SELBY BOTANICAL GARDENS
(Sarasota County)

By all accounts, Bill and Marie Selby were exceptional people. Although rich, their interests and demeanor were modest. In the early 1900s, Bill Selby took his young bride on a touring trip across the entire U.S. His roadster was specially equipped and carried camping gear. Certainly, Marie Selby was one of the first women to travel across the U.S. in a touring car. When her husband brought her to Sarasota, she fell in love with the area, and they built a two-story Spanish-style home. Upon her death in the early 1970s, she willed her home and botanical gardens to be open to the general public. Since the gardens opened in 1975, they have become a world-renowned education and research hub. Of special interest are the epiphytes (air plants) and orchids. In Sarasota on I-75, exit west on SR-780 and proceed to US-41 and go south. After passing through the center of town, prominent signs guide the visitor to the gardens located at 811 South Palm Avenue.

MERRICK HOUSE and Garden Museum
(Miami-Dade County)

The Coral Gables Merrick house, at 907 Coral Way, was the childhood home to George Merrick, founder of Coral Gables. From this once tiny wooden cabin, Merrick envisioned an exotic Mediterranean-style city sprouting from the family's growing citrus farm. By the early 1920s, Merrick's planned community featured wide, winding roads bordered by trees, elaborate entrances, and a massive Venetian pool. By 1925, at the height of Florida's building boom, Merrick sold more than $100 million in property. By 1935, however, his dreams of completing the "City Beautiful" disappeared in the wake of two major hurricanes and the Great Depression. The house has since been restored to its 1920s appearance and features artifacts of a true Florida pioneer, From I-95, take exit 3A to merge onto Dolphin Expy/SR-836 West toward Airport/Medical/Civic Center. Follow SR-836 about 4 miles and take the NW 42nd Avenue South/Le Jejune Road South exit. Merge onto NW 42nd Avenue/North Le Jejune Road/SR-953 S. Follow SR-953 S for 2 miles then turn right at Coral Way/Miracle Mile. Continue following Coral Way to 907 Coral Way.

MONASTERY OF ST. BERNARD
(Dade County)

The ancient 12th century Monastery of St. Bernard de Clairvaux has been called "the world's largest jigsaw puzzle" and "the oldest building in the Western Hemisphere." Saint Bernard Monastery was built in 1160 in Sacramenia, Segovia, Spain, and rebuilt here centuries later. Originally named in honor of the Blessed Mother, it was first called "The Monastery of Our Queen of the Angels." When Cistercian Monk, Bernard of Clairvaux, renowned church leader, became officially recognized as a Saint, the Monastery assumed his moniker, Bernard of Clairvaux.

For 700 years it was home to Monks before it descended into a lower use as a granary. In 1925, William Randolph Hearst, who had become famous with his newspaper's coverage of the Spanish-American War, purchased the Monastery, removed it, and reconstructed it in Miami. Dismantled stone by stone, each stone was assigned a number, and this mother lode placed into 11,000 wooden boxes lined with hay for packing insulation. As luck would have it, a "hoof-and-mouth" outbreak happened about the same time in Europe, spreading panic that the packing material in the crates would transport the disease to America. The boxes thereupon were pried open and the hay torched, removing one possible carrier of the disease. Meanwhile, Hearst's Empire took a downhill turn as the Great Depression loomed. The stones languished in a warehouse for 26 years. After Hearst's death in 1952, entrepreneurs William Edgemon and Raymond Ross envisioned a rebuilt monastery as an attraction and bought the stones. Twenty-three men labored 90 days opening seven tons of boxes. The Episcopalian Dioceses of South Florida acquired the land in 1964. When financial problems beset the Dioceses, the monastery was purchased by philanthropist Col. Robert Pentland, Jr., and given to the Parish of St. Bernard de Clairvaux. The gardens are designed to represent early Segovia of the 1100s. The Cloisters and Monastery are located at 16711 West Dixie Highway, North Miami Beach.

▽ *A tiled hallway at the Monestery of St. Bernard.*

▲ *Hamilton Disston purchased four million acres of South Florida in 1881. He is known for his efforts to develop South Florida's agriculture and cattle ranching and intended to drain the Everglades in order to achieve his goals.*

OKEECHOBEE WATERWAY

(Glades, Hendry, Lee, Martin, Okeechobee, Palm Beach, and St. Lucie counties)

In modern times, many boats travel from the Atlantic to the Gulf, or vice versa, through the Okeechobee Waterway, which passes through Florida's largest lake, Lake Okeechobee. The waterway is thought of as the Caloosahatchee and St. Lucie rivers. However, this was not the original intention of Hamilton Disston, a northern industrialist, who had one of those "Florida moments" that altered the landscape forever. In 1881, Disston bought 4-million acres of swamp and land in South Florida. He paid a million dollars to the state, about 25 cents an acre. Likely he saved the state financially, as it was broke. Disston dreamed of connecting the St. Johns to Lake Okeechobee and Lake Okeechobee to the Gulf. Down this route his ships would sail. He also envisioned draining a large part of

what are now the Everglades and turning it into cattle pasture. In those days, the Caloosahatchee River originated at Lake Flirt, near modern day LaBelle. It was not connected to Lake Okeechobee. Between Lake Flirt and Lake Okeechobee was land. Through this land, Disston dredged a canal. At Lake Flirt, he had a rare Florida waterfall dynamited out of existence. Okeechobee was thus connected to the Gulf and the Atlantic. The topography of South Florida and the Everglades was altered forever. Disston's projects generally did not fare well in Florida. The waterway was later widened by the Corps of Engineers into the canal it is today. It is possible to hike around Lake Okeechobee as part of the Florida Trail and boat down the waterway. Florida's greatest lake, put in prison by dikes for flood control, can be accessed from US-441 to its east, US-27 to its south, and SR-78 on its west side.

▲ *Flagler College.*

PONCE DE LEON HOTEL/FLAGLER COLLEGE (St. Johns County)

As one of America's wealthiest men, Henry Flagler's determination to convert St. Augustine into a wintering paradise for wealthy northerners was insatiable. His first action, once railroads and steamboats provided access, was to construct the finest hotel imaginable. And in 1888, he did

just that. Considered the largest, poured-concrete structure of its day, the Spanish Renaissance revival-style hotel bathed its guests in opulence and electricity, thanks in part to master craftsmen like Louis C. Tiffany and Thomas Edison. Although operating as part of Flagler College since the late 1960s, the Ponce remains a true historic landmark to Flagler and the transformation

of modern Florida. From I-95, take Exit 318 east (SR-16) toward St. Augustine until it intersects with US-1. Turn right and then left on King Street. Flagler College is located .5 mile east of US-1 on King Street.

➤ *Flagler College.*

53

⋏ *The facade of the Ringling home, Ca' d'Zan, or "House of John." This view shows the side of the mansion facing Sarasota Bay and the tiled patio.*

RINGLING MUSEUM OF ART

(Sarasota County)

The name inspires imagination: "The Ringling Brothers Barnum and Bailey Circus." In the circus heydays, the train pulled into town and the roustabouts erected tents. Elephants and tigers performed with acrobats and jugglers and little folk. The circus brought a wild excitement to town. Originally there were five Ringling brothers, but three succumbed during the decade between 1910 and 1919. In time, John Ringling, who outlived his other brother, Charles, controlled all the major circuses in North America. The Great Depression rocked America, and Ringling himself was voted out of control of the corporation in 1932. He died in 1936. But, his legacy lives on in many ways. It is impossible to think of a circus without thinking of the Ringlings. He left the Ringling Museum of Art behind; it is the official art museum of Florida. It has 21 galleries and paintings by the masters. The museum includes American, Asian, European, and Cypriot works of art, including contemporary art. The Historic Asolo Theater became part of the museum when a forward-looking director purchased a building once owned by an exiled Cypriot Queen, Caterina Cornaro. The house, built in Asolo, Italy, was restored before it became part of the museum in the late 1940s. Drama and comedy presentations began in the theater in 1952, and a large modern theater complex now also entertains visitors. Located on spacious grounds overlooking Sarasota Bay, the Ringling is a west turn from I-75 in Sarasota onto University Parkway, a road reaching the Ringling and Asolo grounds at US-41.

CA D'ZAN MANSION

When John Ringling was a humble circus promoter of modest means, he envisioned himself rising through the circus ranks to become one of America's premier devotees of the arts. Keeping his dream alive, by the 1920s, he had accumulated extreme wealth from the circus, as well as investments in oil, railroads, and other ventures. Along with his adored wife, Mable, he became enamored with world travel and bought back masterpieces of art and furniture from Europe. Deciding upon Sarasota on Florida's West Coast to spend his winters, he built a Venetian Gothic Mansion like no other to house his collection of art and furnishings. Ca d'Zan, which in the Venetian dialect means "the house of John," took two years to complete. It was begun in 1924 and completed by 1926, just before Florida's land bust. It cost a million dollars. Designed by New York architect Dwight James Baum, the two-story structure looks gracefully upon Sarasota Bay from its 66 original acres. Adorned with fancy terracotta work, the stately house is crowned with a majestic belvedere tower, designed to incorporate an electro-magnetic organ in the living room. This organ could send beautiful music into each of the mansion's 51 rooms. When John Ringling died in 1936, he had $311 in his pocket. Cleverly outwitting his creditors, he bequeathed Ca d'Zan to the State of Florida, and it became the state museum.

▲ *The Sunshine Skyway's name was chosen through a contest open to the public. This bridge greatly shortened the journey from St. Petersburg to the communities to the south along Florida's Gulf coast.*

SUNSHINE SKYWAY BRIDGE

(Hillsborough, Manatee, and Pinellas counties)

Until the construction of the original Sunshine Skyway across Tampa Bay, either travelers took a ferry on a long, slow trip across a busy shipping channel or they drove around Tampa Bay, a considerable distance to reach Manatee and its neighbor to the south, Sarasota. When the bridge was first completed in 1954, the top was a steep cantilever truss; drivers and their passengers could look through openings to the ocean 150 feet below. The mesh on the center span often slightly wobbled automobiles, making the ride exciting to say the least. On the morning of May 9, 1980, a freaky wind came from the west. If you lived in a house with the windows open, your drapes suddenly rose with a howling wind. It is speculated that this unexpected gust tossed the freighter Summit Venture into a pillar of the Skyway. By then the original two spans had been widened to four. The freighter was built in Japan four years earlier and displaced nearly 20,000 tons. Approximately 85 feet wide and nearing 600 feet in length, the vessel smashed into the bridge sending vehicles and a Greyhound bus over the edge and into the brink. Thirty-five lives were lost, and only one man who made the fall survived; his vehicle landed atop the Summit Venture. The replacement bridge is said to have had its design inspired by a bridge seen by Florida's former Senator and Governor, Bob Graham. The new bridge is 5.5 miles long and helps cover the same 15-mile path, but it is higher at 193 feet and has a cable-stayed main span. It is the longest bridge of this design in the world. In recognition of Bob Graham, the new bridge was designated The Bob Graham Sunshine Skyway Bridge. If Florida attracts dreamers, tall bridges attract those with nightmares. The number of people who have jumped to their deaths from the new bridge since it was completed in 1987 presently exceeds 150. Like the San Francisco Bay Bridge, the Skyway attracts unfortunates wanting to end it all. The new Skyway has nearly three times the number of suicides than the old bridge. Despite what jumpers might think, this is not a pleasant death, and is like riding on the hood of a car into another car at 75 mph. Please don't do it. Get help, as we are all precious; the Florida dreamers may have nightmares, but they always wake up. The bridge is part of I-275 stretching through Hillsborough County and going across the bay on the Howard Franklin Bridge. I-275 shoots through Pinellas County to rejoin I-75, which it departed from at the northern Hillsborough County line, in Manatee County. It is a wonder to look at the Skyway, and it is a widely recognized symbol of the Tampa Bay area.

⋏ *This dredge and similar equipment was used to create drainage canals as roads were built through swampy areas and to help construct the Tamiami Trail.*

TAMIAMI TRAIL (From Tampa to Miami, US-41)

The state intended to build the Tamiami Trail but ran out of money. To the rescue of The Tamiami Trail came Barron Collier. He was not a Baron; rather Barron, with two 'r's,' was his first name. This man who was born in Memphis, Tennessee, in 1873, completed the roadway on condition that Florida would name a county for him. Today Collier County bears his name. It was a tough stretch of road from Naples to Miami, passing through the Everglades, and a land populated both then and now by countless mosquitoes. Finished in 1927, the section that Collier funded cost $8 million dollars, or $25,000 a mile. This was an astronomical cost in those days. Collier earned his wealth through advertising card franchises. More than 70 affiliates of Collier handed out promotional advertising at trolley and train terminals. The road that was ripped through the almost impenetrable Everglades was made possible by a machine called "a walking dredge." The walking dredge can be seen at Collier-Seminole State Park along US-41 south of Naples. Collier County has an excellent museum system, consisting of Collier County Naples Museum and outlying museums (see final chapter and Appendix A). The construction of the "trail" changed the lives of many formerly reclusive Seminoles. In addition to all the commerce and growth generated by the "trail," Seminoles embarked into the tourist business.

TONY JANNUS PARK AND PLAQUE

(Hillsborough and Pinellas counties)

A City of St. Petersburg historical marker is located a bit to the north of the Pier approach in St. Petersburg on Second Avenue Northeast. This plaque commemorates Florida's "Kitty Hawk," the first regularly scheduled commercial airline flight from Jannus Park from St. Petersburg on New Year's Day, 1914. The pilot was Antony "Tony" Jannus, who was flying a Benoist bi-plane (a replica is nearby in the St. Petersburg Museum of History). Jannus had one passenger, St. Petersburg Mayor Abe Phiel, and one bag of mail. Achieving an altitude of only 15 feet, Jannus flew to Tampa across old Tampa Bay and into aviation history. From I-275 in St. Petersburg, take I-375 east and exit downtown. Due to one-way traffic, some twisting and turning is necessary to arrive two blocks north of Central Avenue on the water where the Pier complex is located.

Tony Jannus Park in Tampa is located at 200 Bayshore Boulevard in Tampa. From I-275, take the downtown exit and proceed to Kennedy Boulevard and turn west. Go across the bridge and turn south on Hyde Park and proceed to Bayshore. Turn right on Bayshore and go to 200 Bayshore Boulevard.

⋏ *A model of the Benoist airplane used by Tony Janus hangs in the St. Petersburg Museum of History.*

⋏ *The beautiful Vizcaya mansion charms visitors with its Italian Renaissance styling.*

VIZCAYA HOUSE and Gardens
(Dade County)

Vizcaya was completed in 1916 as a winter retreat for James Deering, co-founder of International Harvester. More than 1,000 laborers and craftsmen were employed to construct the lavishly decorated, Italian Renaissance estate overlooking south Miami's Biscayne Bay. Following Deering's death and hurricane damage in 1926 and 1935, most of the vast estate was sold to developers. However, Dade County acquired the main house and furnishings in the 1950s as a public museum. Guests can stroll among 400 years of original European antiques and artwork in the main house, as well as ten acres of sculptures, statues and fountains in the formal gardens. From I-95, take Exit 1A. Turn right onto South Miami Avenue. At the third light, turn left into Vizcaya.

VENETIAN POOL (Dade County)

Believed to be the only swimming pool to be included in the National Register of Historic Places, Coral Gable's Venetian Pool was completed in 1924. The pool features waterfalls, three-story observation towers, and a rock diving platform. Originally a limestone quarry pit, the pool holds over 800,000 gallons of artesian well-fed water. Favored by the rich and famous over the years for its exotic setting and cool clear waters, the Venetian Pool continues to draw crowds exceeding one hundred thousand yearly. From I-95 South, merge onto US-1. Turn right on Bird Road for a few blocks then turn right on Granada Blvd. Proceed north for 16 blocks to the fountain.

⋏ *The Venetian Pool in Coral Gables.*

WAKULLA SPRINGS STATE PARK
(Wakulla County)

This wonderful state park could be easily placed in any portion of this book. Certainly before there were Floridians, the area of the spring was home to early and extinct mammals, including mastodons, whose bones are on display in the lodge reception area. The springs are a natural wonder, and it is Florida's premier first-magnitude spring. Early Native Americans, the Apalachee, lived about in the vicinity. For the purposes of this history book, however, it is necessary also to mention the man who preserved this site and used it as a lodge. This remarkable man was politically strong enough to influence the selection of governors and senators. His name was Ed Ball. The state park, with its incredible springs, boat tour, trails, and lodge is south of Tallahassee on SR-267.

➢ *A diver holds part of the lower jaw of a mastodon recovered from Wakulla Springs in 1933. In many of the large, freshwater springs located throughout the state, archaeologists have found evidence of prehistoric human activity, such as stone tools like spearpoints dating from the ancient past when mastodons, mammoths, saber-toothed tigers, and other large mammals still walked through Florida and swam in and drank from its springs.*

ED BALL AND THE ST. JOE COMPANY

Ed Ball once mined for gold in Alaska. He found it in Florida in an altered form. His sister, Jessie, married Alfred I. DuPont. Among the DuPont's family's vast holdings, were those in Florida, primarily in Franklin and Gulf counties. Alfred DuPont put his brother-in-law in charge of the Florida fortunes, and it was a very good thing for the DuPont family. When DuPont died in 1935, he left Ed Ball in charge through a charitable trust, which remains in effect to this day.

During the 1920s and the Depression, Ball bought up land on the cheap. He bought up so much land that at one time the company owned more than 1 million acres in the north and northwest (it now owns less). Ball built a pulp mill in Port St. Joe and harvested out all the longleaf pine he could find, forever altering the environment. His pulp mill needed water, 35 million gallons or more a day, and so he had a canal dredged to the Chipola River when local water sources were not enough. In the place of ancient longleaf pine, he planted commercial slash pine; the devastation of the original longleaf pine forests negatively impacted a number of creatures, including the now endangered red-cockaded woodpecker. His efforts led to the purchase of the Florida East Coast Railroad.

He was obviously a good businessman, and he has left the public the lodge he built. He liked to hunt and drink bourbon and was known to offer a toast of "Confusion to our enemies." One of his enemies was U.S. Senator Claude Pepper. Congressman George Smathers, the man who eventually beat Senator Pepper out of his Senate seat, was a protégé of Pepper who had promised never to run against him. Ed Ball encouraged Smathers to break that promise. Pepper, a Roosevelt Democrat and New Dealer, was in favor of labor unions and other New Deal programs, and thus incurred Ball's displeasure. Ball had a number of disputes with unions.

The odorous pulp mill in Port St. Joe no longer runs. It has left behind pollution problems. The enormous timberland owned by St. Joe Company is being turned into real estate developments; some of it, like a nearby airport and communities north of Panama City are quite controversial.

WHITEHALL/HENRY MORRISON FLAGLER MUSEUM

(Palm Beach County)

Henry Flagler built Whitehall in 1902 as a wedding present for his wife, Mary Lily Kenan. Built as a monument to the Gilded Age technology and as a home for the works of arts and literature, it was Florida's first museum. Upon completion, the *New York Herald Times* proclaimed Whitehall "more wonderful than any place in Europe, grandier (sic) and more magnificent than any other private dwelling in the world." The home was designed by New York architects Carrere and Hastings, who were responsible for many other American Beaux Arts masterpieces, including a U.S. Senate building, the Frick Collection, and the New York Public Library. At an age when most would have retired, Flagler stepped back from his daily responsibilities as a founding partner in Standard Oil to pursue his interests in Florida—from Jacksonville to Key West, a series of luxury hotels and 2 million acres for agricultural development.

△ *The dining room at Whitehall has been preserved and is accessible to visitors today.*

Flagler literally invented modern Florida and established tourism and agricultural as the backbone of the Florida economy throughout the 20th century and into the 21st. Today, Whitehall is a National Historic Landmark celebrating its 50th year as the Henry Morrison Flagler Museum. From I-95, take Okeechobee Boulevard/SR-704 exit east to Palm Beach. Follow SR-704 over Royal Park Bridge and take a left at Coconut Row for a few blocks. Turn left at Whitehall Way.

▽ *Flagler's personal rail car.*

▽ *Whitehall, the home of Henry Flagler, photographed shortly after its construction was completed in 1902.*

Λ *Shamu, the famous killer whale, was the star attraction at Sea World, Orlando, for many years.*

In the earliest days of tourism in Florida, travel for recreation was the province of the rich. While most Americans struggled to earn a living, the elite experienced vacations by steamboat down the St. Johns River into the Ocklawaha and up the Silver River to enjoy Silver Springs. Steamboats were a dominant form of transportation, along with the trains. While few modern Americans would try it, Mark Twain even traveled to Europe on a steamboat, an event detailed in *The Innocents Abroad*.

Before World War II, 20th Century tourism's driving forces were fishing, hunting, and Florida's fabulous beaches. After the Great Depression, World War II, and the advent of the automobile, the middleclass Americans felt entitled to a summer vacation with their children. They still do.

With the growth in air travel, national and international flights soon brought tourists, including Canadians, northern Americans, Asians, South Americans, and Europeans. Along with agriculture and development, tourism has been a driving economic force in Florida. Tourism has also brought many new Floridians, whose pleasant experiences on a vacation inspired a move to Florida, often from across the continent.

BELLEVIEW BILTMORE HOTEL

(Pinellas County)

While Henry Flagler was developing the East Coast of Florida, Henry Bradley Plant was envisioning Tampa and the West Coast of Florida becoming a destination for America's elite. Few had a keener vision than Plant when in 1896 he spied a high bluff in Belleair. "Here I will build my West Coast Hotel." Until recently, the Belleview was the "world's largest, occupied wooden structure." The "White Queen of the Gulf" opened its doors on January 15, 1897, with 100 rooms. When Henry Plant died before the hotel was finished his son, Morton F. Plant, took the helm in 1900. It was placed on the National Register of Historic Places

The Belleview Biltmore shortly after its construction. Note the siding for private rail cars.

in 1980. The Plants found taxes lower than in Clearwater and set out to build a model city with the multi-gabled Victorian hotel and the nearby Victorian cottages for winter guests who desired more privacy on the 625-acre parcel. An early feature was an asphalt, circular bicycle track on which International Championship races were held. By 1916, American golf architect Donald J. Ross completed an 18-hole course. An east wing came in 1902, including the main dining room and kitchen. The south wing was added in 1926 and the hotel was doubled in size. There are four and five stories under two and one half acres of roof and two miles of hallways. In recent years, the Belleview

was almost lost as the massive structure was declared functionally obsolete. However, preservationists fought and helped save (at least temporarily) one of few remaining grand hostelries in the country. Today, noted architect Richard J. Heisenbottle along with the Legg-Mason Company and Skanska Construction are set to bring back the hotel to its glory with a massive 5-year restoration plan. During World War II, the Biltmore found use in the great patriotic effort by billeting soldiers. From US-19 in Clearwater, exit west on SR-60. Turn south on Fort Harrison and proceed to entrance to Belleair. Make a west turn and follow the road to the entrance to the hotel.

THE SON OF THE FATHER

Morton F. Plant was known for his sailing and sportsmanship long before he took over the reins of his father's empire. He had a son, Henry Plant, II, who was injured on the Biltmore grounds in a car accident. Plant had to send a car to Chicago to bring a specialist to Clearwater to tend to his son. After that experience, Morton Plant donated $100,000 to start a hospital, known today as Clearwater's Morton Plant Hospital.

After Morton's wife Nellie died, Morton was inspecting a trolley line he owned in Waterford, Connecticut, when he happened to spy Sara Mae Caldwell-Manwaring. The woman was

affectionately called Masie but married to one Seldon Manwaring. History and legend now depart. During tours of the Belleview Biltmore, the tour guide told a tale in which Morton offered Manwaring millions of dollars to let Masie go. History books record that Seldon was caught in a compromising position shortly after Plant became interested in Manwaring's wife; whether this event or its detection had any connection to Morton Plant, no one knows. Whatever the truth of it may be, Manwaring divorced his wife Masie, who promptly married Morton Plant.

Truth and legend may or may not diverge on the following story. When Plant

married Masie, he gave her a building at Fifth Avenue and 52d Street in New York, a mansion where Plant stayed when in the city. Sometime later, Masie turned her eyes on a string of pearls she just had to have, but the price tag was $1.2 million dollars. Tour guides say that when Morton Plant balked at the price of the string, Masie traded the house, now known as the headquarters of Cartier's, for the pearls. History books just record sales and deeds. When Morton Plant died, he left Masie a fortune estimated at $50,000,000.

Λ *Tarpon fishing has lured many sports anglers to Florida.*

BUSCH GARDENS (Hillsborough County)
and SEAWORLD (Orange County)

When Busch Gardens first opened, it gave folks the chance to stroll leisurely around its famous gardens built about its brewery and witness a spectacular bird show, then sit and rest over a cold glass of free Busch beer. My, how things have changed! In 1965, a "Serengeti Plain" was created over which visitors could view African animals from a lift. The "Dark Continent" evolved to have over 2,700 mammals within its confines. The current Busch Gardens combines African safaris with heart-stopping roller coaster rides, as well as many forms of family amusement and zoological displays. Busch Gardens has grown to such a size that a mere day might not be sufficient to experience all its attractions. Moreover, there is a Busch Gardens in Europe and in Virginia (other Busch Garden locations in California and Texas have closed). Busch Gardens is located on Busch Boulevard in Tampa. Busch Boulevard is an exit of I-275. Exit from I-275 east and proceed to 40th Street, then turn north. I-275 can be reached from I-4 if traveling toward Tampa by turning north on I-275. Anheuser-Busch also owned Sea World off I-4 in Orlando. In 2008, Anheuser-Busch was sold to a European beverage company, and the fate of the Garden' ownership remains unclear.

GOLF IN FLORIDA

Florida's mild climate allowed northerners to play golf year round. Thus, many fine golf courses were constructed, and the game no doubt contributed to Florida's rapid growth.

ⵊ *Golf star, Arnold Palmer, and TV star and avid golfer, Jackie Gleason, clown around on a Florida golf course.*

ⵊ *Rosie the elephant being used as a golf tee: Miami Beach, Florida (1927). Developer and entrepreneur Carl Graham Fisher used the elephant Rosie to promote Miami Beach during the Florida land boom of the 1920s.*

ⵊ *Babe Ruth and the former governor of New York, Al Smith, playing a round of golf at the Miami Biltmore, Coral Gables (1930).*

In addition to its beautiful gardens, Cypress Gardens became famous for it thrilling water-ski shows performed on its lakefront.

CHALET SUZANNE (Polk County)

Each of the 26 rooms at Chalet Suzanne Restaurant and Country Inn are uniquely constructed from original horse stables, chicken coops, tool sheds and such. As you can imagine, all are different and have hosted guests on vacation or on romantic retreats. In the beginning, Bertha and Carl Hinshaw, Senior, partnered with J. L. Kraft, of Kraft Cheese. The pre-Depression intention was to found an upscale community; however, these plans were abandoned when the Depression struck and Kraft withdrew from the project. In 1931, when Carl passed away at the age of 47, Bertha decided to create the chalet, naming it after Suzanne, the Hinshaw's only daughter. During World War II, a portion of the Chalet burnt to the ground. Following his service in the Pacific, Carl Hinshaw, Jr., returned to help his mother rebuild the Chalet. In 1956, Carl, Jr., built a soup cannery upon requests from guests who wanted to prepare his soups at home. The soups went way beyond that. The current Chalet includes a soup cannery, begun in 1956; its famed romaine gourmet soup has been served at the World's Fair, in every governor's mansion in the U.S., and aboard manned U.S. spacecraft (aboard Apollo 15 and 16 on their way to the moon and the Appollo-Soyuz joint American-Russian mission).

The Chalet's airstrip is accessible for those with private planes. The award-winning restaurant features such delights as the soup and a sugarcoated, broiled grapefruit. Potential visitors should consult the website for pricing and availability. From Tampa or Orlando, take I-4 to US-27 south, then turn east on Chalet Suzanne Road.

THE CITRUS TOWER AND MUSEUM (Lake County)

Clermont is named for a city in France and the company that established the city in Florida. The lands about Clermont could be called Florida's highlands, although folks in the Rocky or Smokey mountains might find this amusing. The modestly elevated lands are part of the extensive ridge system of Florida and were islands in the last geological epoch. Atop these Florida "hills" stands the Citrus Tower, built in 1956, and according to the website standing "500 feet above sea-level." With its attached gift shop, this was an early Florida tourist attraction. The view from its glass-enclosed observation deck yields vistas of numerous lakes and the gently rolling "hill country." The Citrus Tower can be seen long before arrival. It towers on US-27 north of I-4 and south of US-91.

CYPRESS GARDENS (Polk County)

Just the name "Cypress Gardens" inspires visions of water skiers performing amazing acrobatics and women in antebellum dress. Neither skis nor flowing dresses were especially in the mind of Dick and Julie Pope when they opened their gardens to the public in 1936 in the midst of the Great Depression. Entertaining servicemen in 1943, Dick decided to put on a water-skiing exhibition with his sister and friends; it proved so popular it led to the later famous acts. When a freeze damaged the vegetation at the entrance, Julie hit upon the idea of placing a greeting woman dressed in antebellum finery to divert attention from the dead or dead-looking vegetation. The park changed hands in 1985 and was under the threat of closing as of April 2003. A grassroots effort and a new investor saved Cypress Gardens, which was in its rightful place as one of the state's most popular tourist destination. It suffered badly from three hurricanes running over it in 2004, but was back in its grandeur as before. Now the Gardens have become a Legoland attraction. Cypress Gardens was south of I-4 between US-17 and US-27.

⋏ *A race in progress at Daytona International Speedway.*

DAYTONA INTERNATIONAL SPEEDWAY
(Volusia County)

Florida has long been famous for its white sandy beaches, perfect for sunbathing. However, its most famous beach is known for something else. Dubbed the "World's Most Famous Beach," Daytona Beach has not taken this honor for the squeaky white sand like that found on most of the Gulf Coast. No, Daytona Beach has a different hard-packed sand, not that fancy white stuff. Since the early days, Daytona's beach has conjured up of all sorts of possible uses, including as a makeshift runway for America's first aviators, a place for aeronautical acrobatics, stuntmen and cars, or simply just a fine place for folks to race automobiles. In fact, this was the birthplace of beach racing and early automobile record setting.

While the original time trials started in Ormond Beach, it was Daytona that gained fame for its "measured-mile" races. Before the invention of the combustion engines, the steam-powered cars first raced on Daytona Beach. The Stanley Steamer set the first land speed record there in 1906. For years, a wooden sign on the beach declared: "Exactly 5,280 feet to the south, all the famous speed records have been set." The first record occurred February 26, 1903, when Alexander Winton reached 68

mph. The last record on the sign stated that Sir Malcolm Campbell obtained the speed record of 276 mph on March 7, 1935. By the 1940s, the Daytona races had lengthened and the races were held half on the beach and half on the paved road paralleling the beach route. A group of promoters led by William France, Sr., in 1947 founded NASCAR (National Association for Stock Car Auto Racing). The Daytona International Speedway opened on February 22, 1959, to 41,000 spectators.

Today, the world-renowned, 2.5-mile track configured in a tri-oval, has a seating capacity of 160,000 spectators. The Speedway is capable of hosting everything

from go-kart racing and on and off-road motorcycle events to sport, modified, and stockcar racing. The annual 500-mile race (200 laps) takes place the second or third Sunday in February.

While the Daytona 500 lasts only a few hours, visitors at other times can enjoy the Daytona 500 Experience, where one can get up close and personal by viewing the car that won each year's race, watch a 3-D movie in an IMAX Theatre, or take a tour of the Speedway.

From Melbourne, exit on LPGA Boulevard from I-95. Go east to Clyde Morris Boulevard.

▲ *Harry P. Leu Gardens.*

HARRY P. LEU GARDENS (Orange County)

Located among Orlando's world-famous theme parks, The Harry P. Leu Gardens and Leu House Museum offers a tranquil alternative to the usual rat race. Throughout the romantic 50-acre setting, 3 miles of paved paths lead guests through a variety of vibrant gardens, sculptures, and the Southeast's largest camellia collection featuring over 240 varieties from around the world. At the core of the Harry P. Leu Gardens, among the butterflies, formal rose garden, and moss-draped oaks, is the renovated 1880s plantation-style house of philanthropists Harry P. and Mary Jane Leu. It is listed on the National Register of Historic Places and operated as a house museum showcasing early 20th-century Florida lifestyles. The Leu House was donated along with the landscaped gardens to the city for public use in 1961. From I-4, take Exit 85 (old #43) at Princeton St. and follow the signs.

EVERGLADES WONDER GARDEN (Lee County)

During that social experiment called Prohibition when the U.S. tried to make the brewing, owning, and use of alcoholic beverages illegal (fat chance), the brothers Bill and Lester Piper were allegedly bootleggers in a much colder Michigan. They made their money and moved south to a warmer Florida, and by the mid-1930s Lester had created on 5 acres his "gardens," which consisted of plants and trees he found interesting. His brother Bill was more interested in ranching and land. Lester also began to accumulate a collection of various animals. According to the legend, when people began asking for tours, Lester started charging them. For approximately 75 years as of this writing (2012), Everglades Wonder Gardens has provided up-close glimpses of alligators, crocodiles, and snakes, birds, and mammals, including panthers and bears. In present times, the emphasis is heavy on the animals and short on the gardens. Due to illness in the Piper family and other Pipers who have no interest in running the attraction, the fate of Everglades Wonder Gardens is unknown. It might be sold for development. However, there is hope it will become a publicly operated science center. How well founded such hope may be remains to be seen. Meanwhile, see it while you can. The attraction is located along US-41 in Bonita Springs and can be accessed from I-75 south of Fort Myers by going west on Corkscrew Road, south on US-41, and taking a jog onto Highway 887 south.

JOHN F. KENNEDY SPACE CENTER

(Brevard County)

The first mission at Cape Canaveral took place on July 24, 1950. The base was chosen as launch operations center in 1962. Renamed by President Johnson after the assassination in 1963 of President Kennedy, it is a place where heroes have rocketed into space aboard experimental aircraft. Craft launched under its control have brought back photographs of the planets sufficient to kindle our sense of wonder. The eyes it has sent and maintained in space help us to monitor our weather and national security, as well as to look back in time to that of creation itself. It is also a site of dreamers, who wish to explore our solar system and beyond, and to send humans in flight across space to distant planets. It has shown Americans achievement and debacle, great technological efforts, and heart-breaking events. The center is, of course, named for John F. Kennedy, the assassinated President who set the goal of landing a man on the moon when most of America's rockets seemed to be blowing up on the launching pad, especially whenever televised. Rocket launches, and especially Space Shuttle launches, draw crowds from across the state and the nation to witness the latest explorers. At present, Space Shuttle launches are scheduled to end in 2010 or 2011. The Space Center facilities can be toured. Tours can include a trip to the Air Force Museum at nearby Cape Canaveral

∧ *This display of space vehicles tells the history of the Space Center.*

Air Force Station, an incredible IMAX experience, and program highlights of the Mercury, Gemini, Apollo, Skylab, Space Shuttle, and International Space Station. The historic efforts at Cape Kennedy have inspired movies, books, and the human heart. John F. Kennedy Space Center is on Merritt Island. From Titusville, it is a straight shot across the bridge, and once there, follow the signs. Titusville is an exit of I-95 in Brevard County along the Atlantic Coast. Consult the website for launch information and facility operations.

∧ *Space capsules were used in the earliest days of manned space flight. In the days after the Space Shuttle, they will apparently come back into favor for journeys to the moon and beyond.*

∧ *Shuttle launch.*

∧ *Large alligators are part of the attraction at the St. Augustine Alligator Farm.*

MARINELAND (St. Johns County)

Before the "theme parks" changed the face of tourism, Marineland was the most popular Florida destination in the 1950s. For one thing, it had an excellent location. Before interstates, US-1 was a primary north-south highway. US-1 brought Yankees down the Florida coast as far as Miami and the Keys. At St. Augustine, there were a wealth of attractions, and just south of St. Augustine on A-1A along the beach was Marineland – a magical, beckoning name for adults and children alike. Dolphin feedings were one of the many marine marvels then new to the general public. Marineland was originally created as Marine Studios; it produced underwater life as if it were in its natural settings. The Studios played a role in Tarzan movies, a movie called *The Revenge of the Creature* released in 1955; and in 1981 helped create the first scuba-diving dog, Benji, for ABC's *Benji*. Although interstates have diverted the traffic, Marineland is still a magical visit and can be combined with the numerous historical and tourist attractions around St. Augustine. From I-95 exit east on SR-207 to A-1A and proceed south.

SILVER SPRINGS STATE PARK
(Marion County)

Occupied by Indians, invaded by Spaniards, and overrun with 19th century tourists, Silver Springs has long been a Florida attraction. Beginning with steamboats plying the waters in the 1860s and the invention of glass-bottom boats in 1878, the lush tropical wilderness and gin-clear springs have drawn visitors by the millions. The 350-acre, nature theme park, considered one of Florida's oldest attractions, surrounds seven major spring formations near Silver River's pristine headwaters. The park's popularity soared throughout the late 19th century as tourists clamored to peer into the deep, nearly pure waters of the world's largest artesian limestone spring. A 1916 silent film was Hollywood's first 'discovery' of the area. Since then, dozens of movies and commercials have featured Silver Springs as a backdrop. Silver Springs is to the east of Ocala on US-40, an exit of I-75.

ST. AUGUSTINE ALLIGATOR FARM
(Zoological Park) (St. Johns County)

Founded in 1893 as a collection of captured alligators found on Anastasia Island, the St. Augustine Alligator Farm is one of Florida's oldest attractions. Over the decades, several fires damaged the park, resulting in new ownership and relocations. Along with its expansion in size and status, the park has been featured in television shows, documentaries, and public-education films. The site, located at 999 Anastasia Boulevard, features nearly two-dozen species of crocodilian and a wide assortment of mammal, bird, and reptile exhibits. An accredited zoological park and historic place, the St. Augustine Alligator Farm remains a popular Florida attraction. From I-95, take Exit #318. Turn east on SR-16 to US-1 South. Turn left at CR-214/W King Street. Follow King Street over the Bridge of Lions to Anastasia Boullevard/SR-A1A. Follow Anastasia for about 2 miles to 999 Anastasia Boulevard.

SPOOK HILL (Polk County)

Hills have always been considered an anomaly in Florida. So if you find a hill in Lake Wales where something bizarre happens—like a driverless car begins backing up the hill on its own, then you've discovered Spook Hill. Look for the campy Legend of Spook Hill sign on North Lake Wales Drive. According to legend, Seminole Florida Indian Chief Cufowellax lived on this Central Florida Ridge thought to be an isolated island several million years ago. Receding waters left sand and limestone mounds high and

dry. Nearby Iron Mountain connected the Seminoles spiritually to their Sun God, and their village bordered present day Lake Wales. When a particularly pugnacious bull gator threatened the Seminole's tranquil lifestyle, the combative chief rose to the occasion and made quick work of the evil beast in a violent clash. From this turbulent site, legend says, a small lake was formed where, in time, the Chief was buried. Named Lake Ticowa, the Indians later begrudgingly lost these sacred grounds to early settlers. Postal circuit riders circumnavigating the lakeside

trail would notice their steeds laboring as they moved downhill. This was the first time the place was referred to as "Spook Hill." In the early 1900s, the citrus industry emerged dotting the hilly terrain with orange trees. Sometimes automobiles owned by citrus workers would oddly roll uphill pointed in the opposite direction. From I-4 between Tampa and Orlando, exit south on US-27, and turn east on North Lake Wales. A sign announces arrival at Spook Hill.

⋏ *Diving for the cross at Tarpon Springs is an annual event organized by the Greek Orthodox Church. Young men compete to retrieve a cross tossed into one of the large springs. The winner gets a trophy and a special blessing.*

⊲ *Tarpon Springs celebrates Epiphany, the visit of the Three Kings to the infant Jesus, with its annual cross-diving competition.*

⋏ *A typical wooden boat used for collecting of natural sponges at Tarpon Springs at the riverfront wharf.*

TARPON SPRINGS SPONGE DOCKS

(Pinellas County)

For years known as "the home of the world's largest sponge market" Tarpon Springs still retains its colorful sponge boats, its picturesque riverfront setting, and the traditional customs which have been passed down by those of Greek descent still part of this city's population. The colorful sponge boats, built from patterns handed down by Greek shipbuilders for decades, line the docks along the Anclote River. These boats, painted in reds, greens, blues, and yellows are noted for their seaworthiness and are the perennial target of tourist cameras. The old, Phoenician-inspired boats hint at an industry that has been part of Tarpon Springs history since it was moved here from Key West prior to 1900. Tarpon's sponge industry was begun by John King Cheyney and Gus Corcoris. The offspring of a Philadelphia Quaker with holdings in Florida, Cheyney began to ply the Gulf waters when he heard of a natural sponge industry in Key West. With one eye on family interests, the other searched for sponges. Cheyney began to think of new business opportunities. Founding the Anclote and Rock Island Sponge Company in 1891, Cheyney established offices in Philadelphia and Tarpon Spring and recruited a young, skilled Greek diver by the name of John Corcoris. Cheyney knew

in Corcoris that he had person capable of expanding his interests. Soon other divers began to migrate to Tarpon and brought with them a new mode of sponge diving and new equipment. Rubberized diving gear, heavy copper helmets, and prolonged underwater time with the use of air hoses began to supplant the former diving methods. The old "hook boats," in which sponges were snagged from the gulf waters by long hooks, were no longer the fastest way of extracting sponges from the water. Greater distances were achieved by the boats, which obtained better sponges in deeper waters. By 1905, the sponge industry was prospering in Tarpon Springs. Advertisements were placed in Greek newspapers and word reached fishermen of the many Greek Islands including Kalymnos, the center of the industry in the Mediterranean. Many Greeks seeking opportunities in America answered the call and helped fuel the industry. The Sponge Exchange was founded in 1907 and became the center for evaluating, processing, and marketing of sponges. Up through the 1930s, the sponge industry prospered. The 1940s saw the sponge trade founder as bacteria contaminated the sponge beds of the Gulf. The introduction of the synthetic sponges, higher labor costs, and increased expenses of boat construction didn't help matters. The industry was revived in the 1980s, and today

Tarpon Springs has reemerged as a major leader in the global, natural sponge market. A revitalized market place can found here as the entire cycle from harvesting to the weekly wholesale trade captures the interest of tourists who come here to appreciate this gem of Pinellas County. Tarpon Springs lies between Clearwater and New Port Richey to the west of US-19. In Tarpon Springs, turn west from US-19A onto Dionese Boulevard.

⋎ *A bronze statue of one of the original Tarpon Springs sponge divers with his helmet and diving gear.*

THEATER OF THE SEA (Monroe County)

Established in 1946 in a water-filled quarry dug during Henry Flagler's South Florida building spree, Theater of the Sea is one of the oldest aquatic parks. Featuring a wide array of marine life, the 17-acre attraction's programs and shows are as informative as they are entertaining. While not nearly as academic as nearby research centers, Islamorada's Theater of the Sea offers interactive educational encounters with dolphins, sea lions, and stingrays. For the seafarers, there are snorkeling cruises. Located on Key Largo just south of MM-85 on US 1, the attraction is open year-round.

WALT DISNEY WORLD and EPCOT
(Orange County)

Walt Disney's (the gifted and famous animator and creator of family cartoons) company opened Disney World in 1971 and re-arranged Florida tourism forever. More than a billion tourists have passed through Walt Disney World's gates. Walt Disney World outdraws all the other combined major tourist attractions in the state. The addition of Epcot in 1982 solidified its lead in visitors over the other theme parks and attractions. What does Epcot mean? Nowadays the acronym is so widely accepted that few people remember what Walt Disney meant when he coined the term. EPCOT stands for Experimental Prototype Community of Tomorrow, Disney's then futuristic vision. Born Walter Elias Disney in Chicago, Walt Disney may not have had a happy childhood, but he certainly brought joy to families of the next generation. In the 1950s, kids gathered around the new thing called television to watch the Mickey Mouse Club, one of Disney's best-known creations. His work started with "Alice Comedies" thru Disney Studios. Those comedies were based on *Alice In Wonderland*, a book by Lewis Carroll that has perplexed readers everywhere whether it is truly a child's story or an allegoric flight of fancy. Walt was off and running and never stopped. For his efforts, the world has Dumbo, Mickey, Pluto, and knows Snow White and the Seven Dwarfs, as well as Lady and the Tramp. Disney had some training as an illustrator but was apparently exceptionally talented – and certainly imaginative. Disney World and Epcot are located along I-4 near Kissimmee and prominently advertised and marked with road signs.

WEEKI WACHEE SPRINGS STATE PARK
(Hernando County)

At 403 feet, Weeki Wachee is the deepest spring in the U.S. What's more, the springs are home to world famous "live mermaids." Weeki-Wachee's roots

⋏ *The famous EPCOT "ball" representing "Spaceship Earth."*

⋏ *Drawing an underwater portrait of the mermaids at Weeki Wachi Springs.*

as a roadside attraction date back to the mid-1940s, when a retired Navy swim instructor purchased the spring and devised a method of breathing underwater using air compressors and supply hoses. Free to move about in the springs without scuba tanks, young, swimsuit-clad women entertained as subterranean crowds peered through glass walls into the clear waters. For more than 60 years, Weeki-Wachee's "mermaids" have captivated sightseers and movie goers with their underwater musicals and ballets. The West Coast attraction is located on the west side of US-19, north of Hudson, and south of Chassahowitzka.

Most of us alive today did not experience World War II. The effect of the Japanese surprise attack on Pearl Harbor on December 7, 1941, was to galvanize and unify America --much as the events of September 11, 2001 did. Unlike events in the 21st century, the country remained unified in its war efforts. For the three years after "a day that will live in infamy," America was at war on two fronts and nearly every American was involved in some way. The future of the country and the world was clearly at stake and everyone sacrificed. The panorama of events worldwide is too complex to comprehend. The stories are too many to tell. The efforts of Americans numbered in the millions both overseas and at home. The struggle and suffering worldwide was unimaginable. Goods and fuel were rationed at home to support the military effort, and American industry was unleashed. The war lifted the economy that had foundered since the Great Depression began in 1929. The war effort mobilized millions of young men for military service and brought women into the work place in large numbers and new ways. Although the military services remained segregated until the Korean War, large numbers of African Americans served the U.S. courageously in combat and combat support. Americans of all ethnic backgrounds and class encountered more of their own countrymen and the world than ever before. For Florida, which served as a training base for many services, the war brought widespread exposure to tens of thousands of Americans, who would later come to the Sunshine State to live in the great expansion of the 1950s and 1960s when Florida grew at an astonishing rate.

THE ARMED FORCES MILITARY MUSEUM (Pinellas County)

This 35,000 square-foot museum contains equipment, memorabilia, vehicles, and weapons from America's wars, starting with World War II. The

▲ Patriotic posters, like this one, helped morale during the Second World War.

personal diaries and memorabilia of the late Colonel Leonard J. Schroeder have recently been added to the museum's archives. Colonel Schroeder was a local hero who served during the D-Day Invasion of Europe. On June 6, 1944, U.S. troops and their allies landed on a 50-mile stretch of beach in Normandy, France, and began the liberation of Europe from occupying German forces. More than 160,000 troops directly took place in the invasion. The museum honors them and other brave men and women who had served the country in combat and combat support. From US-19 south of Clearwater, take Ulmerton Road west. The museum is located at 2050 34th Way North between Starkey and Belcher roads.

∧ *A view of "the Don" showing the broad, beautiful beach frontage with its white sand.*

DON CESAR HOTEL (Pinellas County)

Not many people nowadays would associate the luxurious Don Cesar with World War II. However during the war, the hotel was used as a convalescence center for American servicemen, its finest hour. One of the wartime guests was Joe DiMaggio. The hotel, originally intended to have 110 rooms, was completed in 1928 with twice the number at almost three times the original estimated cost of $450,000. The Don was the product of the imagination of Thomas Rowe, who in 1924 bought what is essentially today St. Petersburg Beach for a relatively paltry sum. Rowe meant to leave the Don Cesar (pronounced C-zar) to the staff, but when he died he had neglected this detail in his will. The hotel passed onto his wife and eventually failed. In the 1970s, local preservationists led by June Hurley Young rallied to save the grand hotel, which reopened in 1973. From I-275 in St. Petersburg, take the St. Petersburg Beach exit just north of the Sunshine Skyway Bridge and follow it to its end at the pink hotel originally intended to resemble the Royal Hawaiian. Other famous hotels that billeted troops include the Belleview Biltmore in Clearwater and the Vinoy in St. Petersburg.

∧ *The main entrance approach to the Don Cesar Hotel.*

FLORIDA HOLOCAUST MUSEUM

(Pinellas County)

Genocide (the murdering of a entire people) is unfortunately nothing new to the world. Genocide is as ancient as the Bible and as new as events in Dafur. In recent times, the world has witnessed brutal mass slaughters in portions of the former Yugoslavia as well as in Ruwanda. Compared to the Holocaust, however, all the genocide in history pale for several reasons. The first reason is the staggering numbers of lives taken by The Holocaust over a relatively short period of time. Another reason is the methodical, factory-like approach to the eliminating of people of the Jewish faith as The Third Reich's "final solution" to "the Jewish problem." The elimination of Jews from the world was a goal of Hitler's Germany before and during World War II, and up to the last days of the war when Germany had clearly lost, Jews were still being killed in the extermination camps. Jews weren't the only victims; soldiers from Poland and Russia often met the same fate;

the disabled, gypsies, and homosexuals also were exterminated. While there was heroic (if unsuccessful) resistance to Hitler, the complicity of many German citizens of the time also often seems baffling. (To understand the internal situation in German during the war, read Hans Fallada's classic, *Every Man Dies Alone*.) After all, Germany is the country that gave the world Beethoven and other composers, famous philosophers, and scientists of great note. Genocide by Germans shattered the myth that genocide is something that happened a long time ago or far away in "primitive" countries or a crime committed only by "primitive" peoples." Many victims (especially in the beginning of The Holocaust) were merely lined up and shot en masse. Jewish Europeans were later taken to death camps (such as Auschwitz and Treblinka, both built in occupied Poland). The Jews were led to believe they were taking communal showers when, in fact, they were gassed to death in "showers" in which they were locked with no chance of escape. Everything

of value was taken from the victims, even their gold teeth and shoes, before the bodies were incinerated. As an event of human history, The Holocaust is too expansive and awful for most people to fully comprehend. According to some estimates, 17-million people lost their lives, not fighting, but after surrendering or by being rounded up and murdered. The lowest estimate of the number of lives taking by the Nazis through genocide is 12 million. At least 6-million of the victims were of Jewish heritage. Out of the Holocaust have come works or art and literature attesting to the will of the human spirit in the face of what can only be thought of as overpowering evil. The Holocaust led to the founding of the nation of Israel out of Palestine and to this day has impacted the Middle East in many ways. Misguided opinions have appeared in the press in recent years from individuals who felt the Holocaust was some sort of hoax to justify the creation of Israel; this supposition is preposterous. There is more historical documentation for the Holocaust than for most events in human history. Florida is a state with a large Jewish population, and the Jewish contribution to Florida goes back to early settlements and continues into modern times. Many fled the Holocaust from Europe, and other Jews came to Florida after the war was over, many with the post-war boom. The Florida Holocaust Museum has permanent and changing exhibits that include artifacts, photographs, and works of art from The Holocaust. In St. Petersburg, exit I-275 on I-175. Turn north on 5th Street and proceed to 55 Fifth Street South.

ROEBLING AND HIS ALLIGATOR

Clearwater's great philanthropist, Donald Roebling, designed his amphibious tank, the Roebling Alligator, and built it in his local machine shop. The Alligator was originally conceived to save lives, not take them. After the disastrous 1926 hurricane stranded and killed many people in the Lake Okeechobee and Everglades area, Roebling's father, John, was convinced that many lives could have been saved if rescuers had a vehicle that could cross both land and water to reach the stranded. He underwrote his son to design a vehicle that could carry

20 people yet be light enough to move on water. The first prototype was completed in 1937 and called the "Amtrac." Later dubbed "The Alligator," the historic rescue vehicle turned war machine and underwent several different design and motor changes. Roebling finally settled upon a lighter Alligator powered by a 120 horsepower Lincoln-Zephyr engine. It reached 29 mph on land and almost that speed in the water. The vehicles moved by tractor-like cleats. In the late 1930s, the tank was tested in local waters in the mangroves off Clearwater and Dunedin before seeing wartime action. More than 18,000 were built, and their efficiency was proven in combat. Washington officials offered Roebling over a million dollars for the patent to his invention. He sold the rights to the U.S. for only $1.00. After all, Roebling didn't need the money. He was already a millionaire. Roebling's great-grandfather, John, introduced America to wire rope (or steel cable as we know it today) and made his family rich. John's father, Washington, had built the Brooklyn Bridge. For his war efforts, Donald Roebling was presented a Certificate of Achievement in recognition of "exceptional accomplishment on behalf of the U.S. Navy and of meritorious contribution to the national war effort."

FLORIDA WORLD WAR II HERITAGE TRAIL (Statewide)

The state has established this trail consisting of more than 150 historical sites in 74 cities scattered around Florida. The war against fascism and German and Japanese imperialism took more than a quarter-million of its foot soldiers from the Sunshine State. This is a greater number than the entire population of Florida at the start of the Civil War. World War II brought Americans together in concerted effort like no war since. The sacrifices and efforts of millions of Americans, many of whom trained in Florida and later became citizens of the state, are justly revered for the just cause. More than a half-million WWII veterans have made Florida their home. Information on the sites is available from the resource in the appendix or just Google the trail as spelled above.

A *The Japanese style rock garden at Morikami Museum.*

MORIKAMI MUSEUM AND JAPANESE GARDENS (Palm Beach County)

Visiting the Morikami Museum and surrounding gardens is a wonderful and enchanting experience. The museum hosts changing exhibitions that showcase the art and culture of Japan, while adjacent to it the charming and restful 16-acre Roji-en Japanese Garden features several smaller, individual gardens demonstrating how garden design evolved in Japan over a thousand-year period. All are situated in Morikami Park, named for Sukeji ("George") Morikami who came to America from Japan as a young man in 1906. Morikami left his homeland to join a pioneering community of Japanese settlers known as the Yamato Colony, which once existed between the communities that grew into present-day Delray Beach and Boca Raton. While the colony did not thrive, Morikami remained in the area for the rest of his life, acquiring land that he eventually deeded over to Palm Beach County to become the park that bears his name. During World War II, Morikami was not interned as were other Japanese and Japanese Americans who lived in California and other West Coast states, including some former Yamato colonists who had moved from Florida in the 1920s. Along with 120,000 others of Japanese descent, they were locked behind barbed wire in high desert camps in places such as Manzanar and Minidoka, Idaho. While Morikami escaped their fate, his life nevertheless was disrupted by treatment as a "resident enemy alien": his movements were restricted, his bank accounts frozen, and his business taken over by the U. S. government. For a time, U. S. servicemen were bivouacked at his home to watch over his activities. Other Yamato Japanese still living at the former colony site had lands seized by the government for construction of an Army-Air Corps training base where a new secret technology, airborne radar, was to be tested. Despite the war, life soon returned to normal for Morikami, and he was able to purchase much of the land for the future Morikami Park even before the end of hostilities with Japan. His gift of the property in 1974 was to memorialize the pioneering spirit of the Yamato colonists and to thank the people of his adopted country for the opportunities that he had found here. In Delray Beach, exit I-95 at Linton Boulevard. Travel 4 miles west. Turn south at Jog Road. In .75 miles, the entrance to the park is on the right.

A *Masabel Morikami*

TRUMAN'S LITTLE WHITE HOUSE

(Monroe County)

1945 was a year of once in a lifetime decisions for a U.S. President. Harry Truman became the U.S. leader upon the death of Franklin Roosevelt in 1944 while World War II raged. Few knew at the time if Truman would be up to the task of filling those great shoes. Roosevelt had been president longer than any other. Some youngsters serving in the services could not recall a president before Roosevelt. To say he was a father figure and inspiration to Americans was an understatement. And who, after all, was Harry Truman? For one thing, Truman had failed in the hat business, while Roosevelt was comparatively an American aristocrat. Truman's origins were indeed humble, and he had been plagued all this life by poor eyesight. But Truman was the man who coined the phrase "the buck stops here." In 1945, Truman made the agonizing decision to drop atom bombs on Japan to end World War II. Estimates of U.S. casualties should American invade Japan were given at up to 300,000. First atomic death fell on Hiroshima, and when that did not lead to immediate surrender, an atomic

bomb was dropped on Nagasaki. Moreover, Truman was prepared to drop even more atom bombs if necessary rather than risk the lives of American soldiers in a massive and difficult invasion of Japan. Japan, of course, had attacked America, bringing on war; nonetheless the dropping of the atomic bombs still remains controversial. Many argue that a demonstration would have been sufficient without the loss of life. Also during 1945, Truman and his staff laid plans for the rebuilding of Europe and Japan. General Douglas McArthur, who is remembered for his promise to return to the Philippines and for defying Truman in Korea, altered Japanese society by turning it into a democracy during the occupation. McArthur accepted the Japanese surrender. General Dwight Eisenhower, who had led the European campaign, succeeded Harry Truman as President. It is safe to say that the "little haberdasher" changed the world as much as his predecessor Franklin Roosevelt. Many of Truman's decisions were in progress in 1945 when he visited the Little White House. The house was ironically built the same year that Truman was born. President Harry S. Truman's

Little White House is located at 111 Front Street in Key West. To get there, proceed south on US-1, which soon changes from North Roosevelt Boulevard to Truman Avenue. Turn right on Whitehead Street, the first street after Duval. Parking is sometimes problematic, but can generally be found near the intersection of Greene and Whitehead. Front St. and the Little White House are within a gated community that allows automobile traffic only to residents, most of whom work for the government. Pedestrian access is through a large cast iron gate on Greene St. From there one can follow the signs to the Little White House, a short block away. Only the grounds, gift shop, and two exhibit rooms are open to the public free of charge. For a fee, visitors can take a guided tour of the rest of the building. The facility is still used for ceremonial purposes, and for reasons of national security no photography is allowed inside the Little White House and many other historic sites. The official designation is Truman's Little White House Home and Museum.

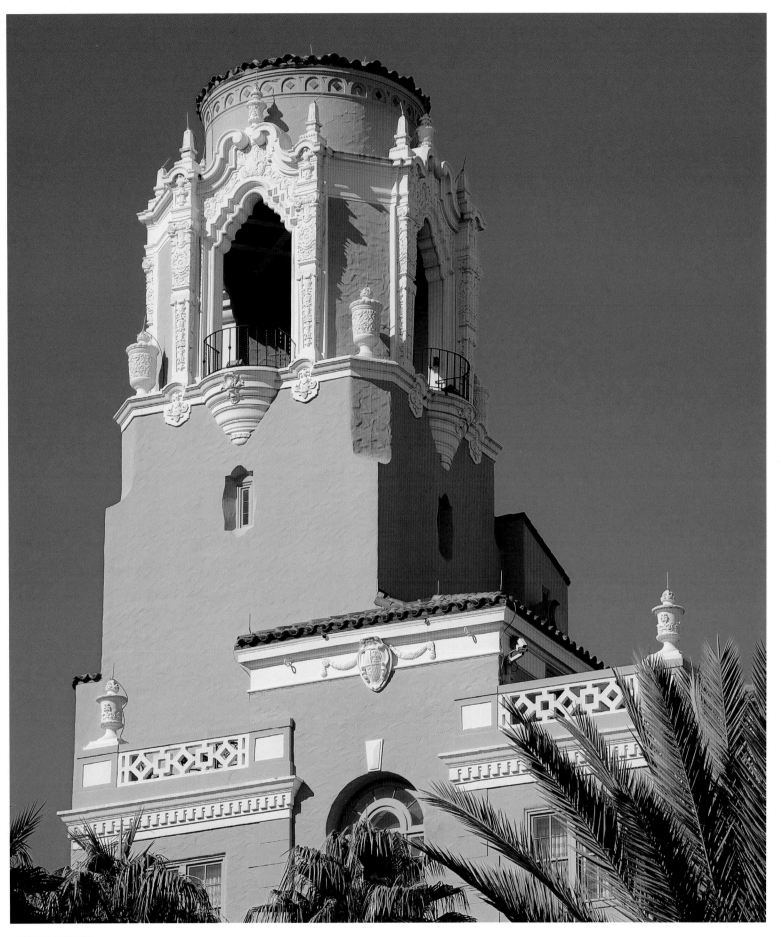

VINOY HOTEL (Pinellas County)

Completed in 1925 for Aymed Vinoy Laughner, the Vinoy's original winter guests included Babe Ruth and two U.S. Presidents (Coolidge and Hoover). During World War II, the Vinoy was a home away from home for Army Air Corps soldiers in training. Florida welcomed the servicemen into many hotels, not only because of patriotism but because Florida was still suffering from the Great Depression. The hotel was sold following the war and closed in 1974, after which it became a haven for the homeless. In the 1990s, the hotel was renovated at great expense and is today a luxury hotel and wedding site for many. It is grand, much like the Don Cesar on nearby St. Petersburg Beach. From I-275 in St. Petersburg take the I-375 exit and go straight to the water. The hotel will be on the left or north side. It is officially the Renaissance Vinoy Hotel or the Vinoy Renaissance Resort and Gulf Club, but to everyone who knows it, it is simply "The Vinoy."

⋏ *Confrontation between black demonstrators and white segregationists at a "whites only" beach at St. Augustine, 1964.*

The 1950s were the crucible of change both in a Supreme Court decision holding that separate schools for the races provided an unequal education (*Brown vs. The Board of Education, Topeka, Kansas*) and in the act of one brave woman. On December 1, 1955, Rosa Parks boarded the public bus that was her normal ride home from her employment in Montgomery, Alabama. Buses in those times in the South were divided into seats for whites in the front of the bus and seats for African Americans in the rear. Mrs. Parks was not actually sitting in the seats reserved for whites but in the middle of the bus, a sort of no-man's land claimed as the bus filled. When due to the seats in the white section of the bus being full a white male could not be seated on the bus, the driver ejected four black bus riders from their seats. Three left their seats, but Rosa Parks refused. An activist, Mrs. Parks was prepared for the consequences, but no one at the time could have foreseen what happened.

Alabama, after all, is not that far from Florida, and the subsequent jailing of Mrs. Parks, the Montgomery bus boycott, and the rise of the Rev. Dr. Martin Luther King shook the segregationist foundation of the South and Florida. Dr. King's evolving tactics were much more effective, as well as dramatic, than efforts in the past by a wide-range of organizations and leaders. Dr. King's campaigns took non-violent principles from those Gandhi and his followers had used in evicting the occupying English Empire from India and merged these tactics with the Christian concept of bearing witness.

The publicity generated by Dr. King's tactics appealed to the good nature of a largely Christian nation that believed all

men could be saved and all souls valuable, as well as to the American concept of democracy, with its belief that all men have rights that cannot be taken away. Positive change was coming. It had been a long time coming and still may not have completely arrived, but Rosa Park's actions and Dr. King's appeal to democratic and Christian values brought struggles and subsequent changes like nothing had before. Students in particular were galvanized.

On a day in May of 1956, two female students of Florida A&M University boarded a Tallahassee city bus and sat in the section reserved for whites. Wilhelmina Jakes and Carrie Patterson were subsequently arrested when they refused the bus driver's order to move. After a struggle lasting about a year, the city buses were integrated. Subsequent efforts to integrate movie theaters in the city that was home to both FAMU and FSU resulted in 257 arrests, and Ku Klux Klan members burned crosses on Tallahassee hillsides.

Demonstrations in St. Augustine in 1964 are credited with helping to pass the Civil Rights Act of the same year. Despite an early history of racial tolerance, St. Augustine was a powder keg in the 1960s. Racially inspired beatings, burning, shootings, and one murder had taken place. Cars of white youths roamed the streets at night. At America's oldest continually inhabited city, Martin Luther King led demonstrators along with Rabbis to a place where they attempted to eat in a segregated restaurant, while a pool swim-in triggered outrage and police reaction.

FLORIDA BLACK HERITAGE TRAIL
(Statewide)

The trail is one of several established by the State of Florida to celebrate its ethnic diversity and history. More than 100 locations are included in the Florida Black Heritage Trail alone. The other state heritage trails include historical sites dedicated to Florida's Cuban and Jewish heritage, women's studies, Native Americans, the Spanish colonial periods, and World War II. Publications describing the locations on each of these trails are available from the Division of Historical Resources (see Appendix A for contact information) and well worth the relatively small fees. Among the stops on the trail are a number of churches, schools, monuments, historic districts, state and federal parks, and homes. The presence of a number of churches in the trail gives testimony not only to the role black churches have historically played in the lives of African Americans but also to their role played during the Civil Rights struggle.

⋎ *Sit-in at Woolworth's lunch counter in Tallahassee, 1960.*

HARRY T. MOORE CENTER
(Brevard County)

The struggle for civil rights in Florida has many silent stories, and such is the case for activists Harry T. and Harriette V. Moore. Employed as teachers in Brevard County in the 1930s, the Moores fought for equal pay for fellow African-American instructors. By 1934, Harry had organized the Brevard County NAACP chapter to further equality and voting rights for African Americans in a racially divided state and in an area that was a bastion of white supremacy. So driven was Moore, he soon secured a top position within the NAACP's Florida Conference. In addition to protesting segregation and disenfranchisement, Harry Moore challenged lynching and brutal police tactics aimed toward blacks. Together, the husband and wife team spent the next decade fighting for human rights, only to become victims. On Christmas Day, December 25th, 1951, their 25th wedding anniversary, the Moore's home exploded. The bombing and assassinations of the Moores was never solved. Located on the family homestead in Mims, the Harry T. and Harriette V. Moore Memorial Park and Cultural Complex commemorates their lives and unwavering struggle for equality and justice.

HEMMING SQUARE (Duval County)

Located in downtown Jacksonville, Hemming Plaza (also called Hemming Square) is the area's oldest public park . The events that took place there were a turning point in the civil-rights movement. On August 27, 1960, 40 activists from the Jacksonville Branch of the NAACP attempted to hold peaceful demonstrations there. Their mission was to stage peaceful sit-ins at the segregated lunch counters at F.W. Woolworth's Five and Ten Cent Store and the W.T. Grant Department Store. Peace however was short lived as 150 whites descended on the demonstrators, clubbing them with baseball bats and ax handles. Many were seriously injured in the event that would become known as "Ax Handle Saturday." Additional demonstrations would occur in the tranquil downtown setting. It would be years before desegregation fully enveloped Jacksonville and Duval County. Today, Hemming Square stands as a reminder of those who risked their lives to ensure a future focused respect to all humans, regardless of the color of their skin. Hemming Square is across from City Hall, located at 117 West Duval Street. From I-95 heading north towards Jacksonville, take the Main Street/Prudential Drive exit. Merge right onto US-1/US-90 for one mile. Turn left at East Duval Street. Follow Duval St. past North Laura Street to the plaza.

⋀ *Ralph Abernathy and Martin Luther King at St. Augustine, 1964. Ralph Abernathy and Martin Luther King were among the founders of the Southern Christian Leadership Conference, a highly significant civil rights organization.*

⋀ *Governor Leroy Collins was known for his moderate views about race relations in a time of racial turmoil.*

GOVERNOR LEROY COLLINS, VOICE OF MODERATION

Like all Southern governors and most elected Southern officials, Governor LeRoy Collins (1955–1961) opposed desegregation as ordered under the *Brown vs Board of Education, Topeka, Kansas* decision of the Supreme Court that eventually ended segregation in public education. When it came to resisting the Supreme Court decision, however, Collins was a voice of moderation, and as Chairman of the Southern Governor's Conference this moderation was felt to some degree throughout the South. During periods of racial tension and violence, Collins was consistently a man urging non-violence and moderation. He attempted (unsuccessfully) to keep the Florida legislature from opposing the Brown Decision through resolution (once by dismissing the legislature under a provision of the state constitution no legislator was aware existed).

In 1961, Collins was Chairman of the Democratic Convention that nominated Kennedy/Johnson. After he left the governor's office in 1961, President Lyndon Johnson appointed Collins Director of the Community Relations Service under the 1964 Civil Rights Act. It was in this capacity that he mediated the crisis in Selma, Alabama. Lyndon Johnson trusted Collins, a fellow Southerner, to walk into the fray at Selma and moderate the climate so that future marchers would not meet the same fate. A photograph of Collins marching with Dr. Martin Luther King, Jr., in Selma, an action he undertook to keep the peace and under orders of a president, was used to defeat Collins when he later ran for the U.S. Senate in 1968.

World War II changed the world – and Florida. For one thing, tens of thousands of Americans trained in Florida and were exposed to its mild winter climate. Following the war, cars were cheap, the GI Bill made home buying possible for all the veterans, and air travel and air-conditioning were perfected. Florida has never been the same since then. In the 20 years from 1970 to 1990, the Florida population grew by 90%, almost doubling. Growth has continued ever since, slowed by economic downturns at times, but relatively unabated, with the first decline in decades noted during the economic troubles of 2008-10. This growth has presented enormous challenges to the natural resources of the state.

The environmental movement in Florida can trace its roots to Governor William Sherman Jennings who served just as the 1900s began. When the general public thinks of Everglades National Park, the name most recalled presently is not that of Mary Mann Jennings, the governor's first lady. Yet, Mrs. Jennings was a woman ahead of her times. She played a role in the creation of a state forestry board; Jennings State Forest northeast of Jacksonville is named for the governor and his lady. She also had a hand in the creation of Royal Palm State Park, which in time became part of Everglades National Park. It should be remembered that this was the time when large populations of birds were slaughtered for their feathers, or plumes, including many within what would become the national park. These efforts also more or less coincided with the election of U.S. President Teddy Roosevelt, whose love for the outdoors led to many conservation efforts.

Jennings's enlightened leadership was followed by different leaders with a very different philosophy. Subsequent leaders for a very long time sought to drain South Florida and convert the land into cattle and agricultural uses. The state was forever altered when Hamilton Disston connected Lake Okeechobee to the Gulf of Mexico through his grand canal, the original skeleton of what is now the Okeechobee Waterway.

During the Great Depression, the Civilian Conservation Corps was created. Within Florida, the CCC built many of the current state parks. The CCC also planted over 13 million trees. The establishment of Everglades National Park in 1947 was a great victory for the natural world, but the boom of the 1950s thru the 90s continued the destruction of the natural order all about the Sunshine State–-and the destruction still continues.

By the 1970s, a national environmental movement had formed. The first Earth Day was held to highlight the destruction of our natural resources and the reordering of the natural world around us. Under President Richard Nixon, the Environmental Protection Agency was formed, and in 1971, the Florida Department of Environmental Protection was created. Emphasis was placed on land conservation and the additional creation of parks.

Florida's environmental problems in current times are staggering in complexity. Urban sprawl has severed wildlife corridors and nearly eliminated panthers (cougars) from Florida while negatively impacting many wild creatures. For each notable success in protecting species, like the salvation of the Key deer population, there are also many setbacks.

The problem, however, is not just a matter of saving animals, but of keeping the quality of the world around Floridians intact. Fertilizers and pesticides have run off into estuaries and traveled into the Gulf and Atlantic. In the Gulf, in particular, these runoffs have enriched the seas with nitrogen and phosphorous, threatening coral reefs, likely encouraging more frequent and longer episodes of red tide, and encouraging sea grass-killing algae blooms. Inadequate wetland setbacks and unrestrained development continue to allow easy access to waterways for such runoff and has put septic tanks in close proximity to wetlands. Many fish species are limited for human consumption because of over-fishing and the presence of mercury, arriving both from runoff and from incinerators. The continual reduction of wetlands reduces the ability to filter out pollutants before they reach the estuaries and seas, and contributes to flooding during heavy rains. Generally, common sense solutions to these problems are opposed by developers who see restrictions as hurting economic growth by raising the cost of housing.

The environmental movement is very much alive in Florida, but often at odds with policymakers, developers, and landowners. The Florida of the 1950s has vanished, and in another 50 years, according to some estimates, Florida will be altered beyond current recognition. Urban sprawl will extend coast-to-coast, north-to-south, and the runoff from our lands will have created dead zones in the seas and decimated coral reefs. One can only hope that all the competing interests in Florida will come to realize what an ecological treasure we still have left and not allow our state to go the way of, say, New Jersey. There is great hope in that we have so much left to protect, and great worry that we will fail to protect what remains.

⋏ *May Mann Jennings, 1872-1963, was the wife of Florida Governor William Jennings. She is well remembered for her efforts to preserve the environment and for many other reforms. She used her network as the head of the Florida Federation of Women's Clubs to rally voters to promote her agenda.*

BISCAYNE NATIONAL PARK (Dade County)

Biscayne National Park, dedicated in 1980, encompasses the southern portion of Biscayne Bay, the northern islands of the Florida Keys, and begins the world's third-largest coral reef. In addition to buffering gale force winds from hurricanes or seasonal storms, the diverse ecosystems protect an abundant array of marine and terrestrial life in a balmy subtropical setting. Teaming with turtles, manatees, and mangroves, 95% of Biscayne National Park's approximately 180,000 acres lies underwater. The park, located roughly 20 miles east of Everglades National Park, is best experienced from watercraft, drawing anglers, kayakers, and swimmers alike. While in the park's boundaries, lighthouse lovers can spot the Fowey Rocks light, located about 6 miles off Key Biscayne. For scuba divers, the park's Maritime Heritage Trail offers glimpses of shipwrecks, with the *Mandalay* a favorite among snorkelers. Even though high winds and humans have destroyed structures on nearby Boca Chita Key, a few stone and concrete structures from a private resort complex constructed in the late 1930s remain for day hikers. And of course there is the Boca Chita "Lighthouse," built by Honeywell. Although most of the half-million guests each year explore Biscayne National Park by boat, visitors can also drive to the park's headquarters at Convoy Point. Once there, park patrons can explore the Dante Fascell Visitor Center and Gallery, take a boat tour, or just simply relax and cast a line out into the exotic emerald waters. Convoy Point can be reached from I-95, the Florida Turnpike, or US-1.

⋏ *A coastal river.*

BLUE SPRINGS STATE PARK
(Volusia County)

Native Americans lived in the area and American botanist John Bartram visited it. Today, Blue Springs is best known for its winter congregations of manatees. At times, concentrations of manatees in the spring run have exceeded 100. Although vigilance remains necessary, the recovery of manatees in Florida is heartening. Latest manatee counts put the numbers at over 4,000. At one time, the manatee population had diminished to under 800 or less. There are also excellent trails to walk, and in the warmer months when the manatees are absent, it is possible to swim in the cooling waters. For manatee viewing, pick any really cold day in fall or winter to visit and be amazed. From I-4 northeast of Orlando, exit south on US-17/92 and go 2.5 miles into Orange City. Make a right on West French Avenue. Manatees can also be easily seen in the colder months at Crystal River National Wildlife Refuge on US-19 north of Homossassa Springs and in that spring run also.

⋏ *Manatee in a spring run.*

⋏ *A manatee photographed from underwater.*

CROSS FLORIDA GREENWAY
(Citrus, Levy, Marion, and Putnam counties)

The ill-fated Cross Florida Barge Canal was poorly conceived and would have damaged the flow of the aquifer from the north of Florida to the south, and many beautiful wilderness areas would have been destroyed. Although President Richard Nixon halted construction in the 1971 because of alleged cost overruns, it was largely through the efforts of an extraordinary naturalist, Marjorie Harris Carr, who galvanized opposition to the project. The canal was intended as a short route from the Atlantic to the Gulf by cutting through the St. Johns River from Jacksonville then entering Ocklawaha River and Withlacoochee River (South) to reach the Gulf above Crystal River. In modern times, portions of the 110 miles can explored by hiking, mountain biking, canoeing, kayaking, or boating. Details on exploring the Cross Florida Greenway can be obtained from the Florida Office of the Greenways (see Appendix A) and at www. floridagreenwaysandtrails.com. The official designation of the trail is appropriately the Marjorie Harris Carr Cross Florida Greenway.

EVERGLADES NATIONAL PARK
(Collier, Dade, and Monroe counties)

To the newcomer, the 1.5-million acre Everglades National Park appears as a foreboding expanse of mangroves, central marsh, sloughs, mosquitoes,alligators, and water moccasins (Florida cottonmouths). In another view, however, it is possible to see the Everglades' waters as home or a wintering ground to several hundred species of birds. Within the confines of the park are a thousand varieties of plants and more than one hundred types of trees. In addition to deer, opossums, and unimaginable numbers of alligators, nearly two-dozen endangered or threatened wildlife species find refuge in the Everglades and the surrounding public land. But the Everglades area is much more than that, as if that weren't already enough. It is a unique ecosystem, the only one of its kind in the world, for it originally was formed by the overflow from a lake.

Dedicated by President Truman as a national park in 1947, this fragile, shallow, and massive wetland covering the southern tip of the Florida peninsula has for thousands of years relied on overflow from Lake Okeechobee and summer rains. Of the historic Everglades, much has been lost; however what remains is protected within the national park.

Marjory Stoneman Douglas wrote the lyric book, *Everglades: River of Grass*. She was one of many who inspired efforts to save the Everglades. For her special role in these efforts, the state headquarters of Florida's Department of Environmental Protection in Tallahassee is housed in the Marjory Stoneman Douglas Building.

These are the entrances into Everglades National Park. One on US-41 leads into Shark Valley. The main park entrance is west of Homestead on SR-9336. Shark Valley conducts bus tours with highly knowledgeable guides and allows the visitor to see about a billion alligators (well, not quite, but it feels like it at times). The third entrance is at the Gulf Coast Visitor Center located at 815 South Oyster Bar Street in Everglades City.

The Homestead entrance leads through a variety of elevation and habitat changes. From the end of the road at Flamingo, it is possible to travel the Wilderness Waterway on the edge of the Ten Thousand Islands.

⋏ *A boardwalk in Everglades National Park leads the visitor to a hammock.*

⋏ *A Seminole airboat tour through the Everglades Water Conservation Area, which is outside Everglades National Park.*

⋏ *President Truman arrives for opening ceremony for Everglades National Park*

⌃ *A variety of waterbirds, such as these Great Blue Herons, can be observed nesting in the safety of Everglades National Park.*

⌃ *Coastal plains willow, a tree commonly found in Everglades National Park.*

FLORIDA PANTHER NATIONAL WILDLIFE REFUGE (Collier County)

On May 31, 2006, while riding a mountain bike in a Central Florida park, the author almost rode over a Florida panther. The animal assumed a submissive posture and crawled to the side of the trail while the stunned author slowly pedaled by. The chances of seeing a Florida panther in the wild, unfortunately, are only a little better than seeing Big Foot. The Florida panther is the penultimate symbol of our vanishing wildlife and wildlife corridors. It is believed that presently around 100 panthers still roam the state, although their numbers have been much less. A population so small does not offer much biological diversity in breeding, but this small population would not exist had not cougars from Texas been imported to breed with their Florida cousins. The Florida Panther NWR exists to assist the survival of the Florida panthers. This noble work is hindered by continued development because Florida panthers need a big range in which to roam and hunt. Although there is a educational trail in a portion of this wildlife refuge, the refuge is dedicated to assisting the panther and education, thus is not open to the public.

HURRICANES

Every year before hurricane season, prudent Floridians stock up food, water, and batteries, while hoping to be spared the wrath of hurricanes. The "season" for hurricanes runs from June 1 to November 30. During this period, the world's oceans heat up and help produce tropical cyclones. Approximately 36% of hurricanes that form in the Atlantic and Gulf impact Florida. The Florida Keys are often in the path of hurricanes even when the storms miss peninsula Florida. Better storm prediction is now possible because of satellites, computers, and an advanced understanding of hurricanes. Some of the most famous hurricanes to impact Florida in "recent" history include The Great Miami Hurricane (1926), The Okeechobee Hurricane (1928), The Labor Day Hurricane (1935), Donna (1960), and Andrew (1992). In 1975, the Saffir-Simpson Scale came into use. Hurricanes are now rated from the weakest (Category 1) to the strongest (Category 5). The habit of naming hurricanes began in the 1950s with the use of the military phonetic alphabet and Hurricane Easy.

➢ *Remains of a bridge after the 1926 hurricane washed the land away from both ends. Photographed at Baker's Haulover Inlet in Miami, Florida on January 25, 1927. Baker's Haulover Inlet is a man-made channel connecting Biscayne Bay with the Atlantic Ocean.*

⋏ *Powerful waves hit the pier at Navarre Beach, Florida, during Hurricane Ivan, 2004.*

HIGHLANDS HAMMOCK STATE PARK
(Highlands County)

This excellent park is a wonderful place to view wildlife and vegetation and includes trails and a walk on a boardwalk across a cypress-dominated swamp. Highlands Hammock State Park may be traced back to 1931 when it became an early example of conservation efforts. In that year, Highlands Hammock became a "cause celebre," as the hammock and cypress swamps were threatened with becoming just another Florida truck farm. These grassroots efforts to save Highlands Hammock were successful. These efforts were championed by wealthy philanthropist, Margaret Roebling, the daughter-in-law of Washington Roebling, who built the Brooklyn Bridge. Other prominent citizens involved in the efforts to save the hammock were Rex Beach, Alexander Blair, and Richard Lieber, among others. Environmental protection was achieved in 1935 when the Florida State Park System was created. Highlands Hammock was one of four original parks. The park had a Civilian Conservation Corps camp, and visitors can observe extensive exhibits showcasing the work of the young men so employed on the park. The CCC planned to establish a Florida Botanical Gardens and Arboretum at a potential cost of $10,000,000 over a period of ten years. The gardens were to be given to the park as trustee, and the lands were merged in 1939. The CCC camp was closed two weeks before Pearl Harbor was bombed. The history of CCC efforts lives on in the state's CCC museum located within the park. Highlands Hammock State Park is located off 27 on SR 634 (Also known as Hammock Road), 4 miles west of Sebring.

JOHN PENNEKAMP CORAL REEF STATE PARK (Monroe County)

The nation's first underwater preserve spans roughly 70 square nautical miles in the Florida Keys. The park encompasses portions of North America's living coral reef. The coral reefs at John Pennekamp Coral Reef State Park were formed by the build up of calcium carbonate skeletons of tiny coral animals. It can take thousands of years to make a reef. The coral-reef structures, among the world's most diverse communities, provide important aquatic nursery grounds and habitats. Several hundred species of fish and invertebrates reside among nearly 60 species of coral within the park's shallow waters. The park was dedicated in 1960 and named in honor of a *Miami Herald* editor and local conservationist. Visitors wishing to get face to face with the park's underwater sights have several options from snorkeling and scuba diving, to canoeing and glass-bottom boat tours. While the park is best appreciated from the water, land dwellers have access to nature trails through tropical hardwood hammock and mangroves, full-facility campgrounds, and the visitor center has a must-see 30,000-gallon saltwater aquarium. John Pennekamp Coral Reef State Park is located in the Florida Keys on US-1 at Mile Marker 102.5.

⅄ *The underwater statue, "Christ of the Abyss," is a magnet for divers at John Pennekamp State Park. It sits at a depth of 25 feet and is one of the most popular attractions at what Sports Illustrated Magazine called "America's first underwater park."*

⅄ *The hawksbill sea turtle is one of five species of sea turtles that may be seen at John Pennekamp Coral Reef State Park. The others are the green, leatherback, loggerhead, and Kemp's Ridley sea turtles.*

⋏ *Beautiful pink Roseate Spoonbills are a common sight at J. N. "Ding" Darling National Wildlife Refuge. They can be easily observed from the scenic auto trail.*

J. N. "DING" DARLING NATIONAL WILDLIFE REFUGE (Lee County)

The cartoonist for whom the refuge is named began his career in 1906 with *The Sioux City Journal* (later, *Des Moines Register*). A frequent target of his cartoons was the wasteful use of natural resources. J. N. "Ding" Darling went on to work for the *New York Globe* and *New York Herald Times*. A leader in the conservationist movement, he created the Duck Stamp. Funds raised from selling the Duck Stamp go to purchasing wetlands and wetlands preservation efforts. The preservation of wetlands is the key to protecting the natural world because wetlands promote life and are involved in every aspect of the environment. "Ding" Darling's efforts led to the creation of Sanibel National Wildlife Refuge, later renamed in his honor in 1967, and he had a major role in the preservation efforts for the Key deer. Floridians in particular and conservationists in general owe a lot to this great man. J. N. "Ding" Darling National Wildlife Refuge contains approximately 6,400 acres in which are seen over 200 species of birds as well as other wildlife and an early Native American mound. The habitat within these public lands includes mangroves, salt marsh, sea grass beds, and hammocks. There are hiking trails and excellent areas to canoe or kayak. In addition, the refuge manages several other wildlife areas nearby. The refuge is on Sanibel Island to the west of Fort Myers. From I-75 in south Ft. Myers, take Daniels Parkway to the toll bridge and cross onto Sanibel. At Periwinkle, turn right and follow the signs.

NATIONAL KEY DEER REFUGE (Monroe County)

In 1955, it was estimated that there were less than 25 Key deer in existence. Key deer are a small subspecies of Virginia white-tailed deer, the kind seen in the southeastern U.S. How small? There are large dogs bigger than some of the deer. There are coyotes bigger than these deer. In 1939, hunting was stopped. Hunting had taken a toll on the Key deer, and it must have been desperation for food, not for sport, for Key deer (although wild animals) are a relatively docile species. But hunting wasn't the only thing plaguing the Key deer. Habitat had been lost, and after hunting was banned, there was poaching. In recent times, the greatest enemy has been the automobile coming along US-1 in the Keys. Since the establishment of the refuge in 1957, the Key deer has become an astonishing success story. How many Key deer there may be is hard to tell because they range outside the 9,200 acres of salt marsh, tropical hammock, and mangroves within the refuge. Certainly there are now well over 600 individuals. There are 17 federally listed species within the refuge that is on the Gulf side of US-1 in Big Pine Key.

⋏ *Flocks of White Pelicans are often seen at "Ding" Darling.*

⋏ Buffalo introduced into Paynes Prairie are difficult for visitors to find and observe, yet they are plentiful enough to sometimes prove an nuisance to nearby residents in modern times.

PAYNES PRARIE PRESERVE STATE PARK (Alachua County)

Just south of Gainesville along I-75, there appears a great, broad marshy expanse east and west of the interstate. This vast, low-lying area is called Paynes Prairie today, but it once was a mammoth lake when Native Americans roamed this neck of the woods thousands of years ago. On the north side of Paynes Prairie there is a high bluff that was once the north bank of the old lake. The lake was drained when a sink opened beneath it. The sink at times dams-up and the prairie floods. Paynes Prairie became Florida's first state preserve in 1971. Biologically, geologically, and historically rich, its significance led to a national landmark designation. William Bartram, America's first native-born naturalist, dubbed Payne's Prairie in his writings "the great Alachua Savannah" when he visited the site in 1774. The visitor center at Paynes Prairie is the best place to begin an exploration. Hundreds of species of birds and over 20 different biological habitats are explained in an informative audio-visual center. Ascension of a 50-foot tower provides a dramatic overview of the entire Prairie. Further experiences at the preserve include long hiking, horseback riding trails, and bicycling trails. From I-75, take exit 374, the Micanopy exit and take CR-234 east to US-441. The Preserve is 0.6 miles north on US-441.

Charles Walker Studio

⋏ *A painting by Charles Walker, one of the Highwaymen.*

Florida has a number of well-known, native-born and migrating artists and writers. Perhaps the first acclaimed Florida writer was William Bartram whose book *Travels* captured the imagination of readers worldwide. Other writers have written of Florida's rich natural endowments: John James Audubon, Marjory Stoneman Douglas, (*Everglades, The River of Grass),* and Harriet Beecher Stowe (*Palmetto Leaves*), among many others.

Key West has a literary tradition all its own. Hemingway's famous attachment to Key West was also shared by Tennessee Williams, John Hersey, Thornton Wilder, and Archibald MacLeish.

While Zora Neale Hurston's works have enjoyed a newfound modern popularity, the literature of Jacksonville native James Weldon Johnson (1874-1938) has largely disappeared into the realm of rare books. Johnson's works deserve a new revival. Johnson composed "Lift Every Voice and Sing," selected as the anthem of the NAACP, and several books, the most noteworthy of which is *Autobiography of an Ex-Colored Man* (1937).

Florida can claim the famous Ray Charles and the infamous Jim Morrison of The Doors. Florida is now part of a circuit for traveling music of every type, from classical to blues, rock, classic, pop, and country.

Florida's painters have varied from the Highwaymen (African American painters who emerged in the 1950s on the lower east coast) to Salvador Dali. Every metropolitan area is now home to an art museum with rotating and permanent galleries.

In the early 1950s, 26 African-American artists became known as The Highwaymen. This was because they would travel the highway to sell their art to interested businesses and individuals. These artists painted on inexpensive Upson board (similar to chip-board) and worked not from studios but from their garages and backyards. The art of the highway is generally bright and vivid and features many typical Florida scenes. Today these paintings sell for thousands of dollars but a typical price at the time of creation was $25. The work of The Highwaymen can be seen in many Florida museums in both permanent and special exhibits.

Jack Kerouac's book *On the Road* had a St. Petersburg connection. Stephen Crane's classic short story "The Open Boat" involved his own shipwrecking off the Atlantic Coast, and he later married a local Jacksonville madam. The beloved novels of Marjorie Kinnan Rawlings were written in Cross Creek, east of Gainesville. Florida is the land of Harry Crews, Carl Hiaasen, and a sometime Sarasota County inhabitant who is a pretty well known writer who might make it some day—Stephen King.

⋀ *Hemingway Home in Key West.*

HEMINGWAY HOME (Monroe County)

It is one of Key West's most popular attractions, and a crowd of visitors often gathers at the entrance. The Key West Lighthouse Museum is across the street at 938 Whitehead. The lighthouse is plainly visible from "Papa" Hemingway's garden. Hemingway was a prolific author whose novels varied from the "lost generation" in Europe (*The Sun Also Rises, A Moveable Feast*), World War I (*A Farewell to Arms*), the Spanish Revolution (*For Whom the Bell Tolls*), bullfighting (*Death in the Afternoon*), and the famed *Old Man and the Sea*, among others. In addition, Hemingway was considered a masterful short-story writer, whose sparse description and bullet-like dialogue was unique. The Ernest Hemingway Home and Museum is located on 907 Whitehead Street in the Old Town district of Key West. To get there, proceed south on Roosevelt Blvd. (US-1), which soon becomes Truman Ave. Turn right on Whitehead St. Visitors are free to roam the grounds or join a guided tour. One of Hemmingway's homes remains in Cuba, but is currently closed to Americans,

as is travel to Cuba. This home contains over 8,000 books owned and presumably read by Hemingway. The current Sloppy Joe's bar, has an annual Hemingway look-alike competition. Another highlight of a visit are the descendants of the many-toed Hemingway cats.

HASLAM'S BOOK STORE (Pinellas County)

Since 1933, Haslam's Book Store has been a St. Petersburg landmark. Its current stock of over 300,000 new, rare, and used books makes it a joy for readers. The list of internationally known authors who have appeared or signed books at Haslam's Bookstore includes a long list of literary giants such as John O'Hara, Salman Rushdie, John Updike, and its is said that the ghost of Jack Kerouac haunts the store. Back when there was Doc Webb's City and The Million Dollar Pier, a visit to St. Petersburg was not complete without a stop at Haslam's to browse their huge selection; thus author Tim Ohr has had the joy of both shopping there as a child and an adult, as well as signing books within the store.

Jack Kerouac became famous for the book *On the Road* that was a sensational look into the world of the beatniks when it appeared in 1957. Kerouac went on to publish many more books before his unfortunate death at the age of 47 in St. Petersburg where he often stayed with his mother and sister. At the time of his death, he was also living with his third wife. Kerouac is said to have influenced such writers as Tom Robbins and Hunter S. Thompson. He certainly influenced the generation of the writers of this book, as has Haslam's Book Store. The Southeast Independent Booksellers Associations had an annual Charles Haslam Award given to the best independent bookstore. Charles and Elizabeth Haslam were cherished members of their community. Alas, they are gone but Haslam's remains. Haslam's is located at 2025 Central Avenue in St. Petersburg, roughly halfway between US-19 and Tampa Bay. As regards the veracity of Kerouac's ghost, several employees of Haslam's have reported the ghost, and at least one quit upon encountering it.

MARJORIE KINNAN RAWLINGS
HISTORIC STATE PARK (Alachua County)

In 1928 during the 9th year of their marriage, the Rawlings moved to a 72-acre farm in Hawthorne. Both Charles and Marjorie were writers; he sought to create yachting stories while she wanted to be a romance writer. Although they planned to write in Hawthorne, they were quickly overcome with work to keep the orange grove producing and with all the chores that came from living in a house without electricity or indoor plumbing. Five years later, Marjorie was a published author, while Charles and the brothers who helped him with the labor were gone. She divorced her husband in 1933 and in 1941 married Norman Baskins, a hotelkeeper. She kept the name Rawlings after she married because by then it was a well-known name. Her most famous novel is *The Yearling* (1938), a novel she never wanted to write, but did write because her publisher pushed the idea. The famous editor Maxwell Perkins (Thomas Wolfe, F. Scott Fitzgerald, and Ernest Hemingway, among others, were writers Perkins developed) insisted she write the book. After *The Yearling,* she is best known for *Cross Creek* (1942), based on her own experiences as a Yankee moving into a land of Crackers. Altogether, she created 12 books in her lifetime. Most folks mispronounce Mrs. Rawlings maiden name. It is not 'kin nan' but ka nan. North of Ocala on US-301, make a westerly turn on CR-325 and proceed to the house that lies between Orange and Lochloosa lakes, which are connected by Cross Creek. From US-441 in Micanopy it is necessary to take CR-346 to CR-325. Prominent signs direct the visitor.

⋏ *Marjorie Kinnan Rawlings (1896-1953) was an author who wrote novels with a rural theme. She is best known for her work,* **The Yearling,** *which won the Pulitzer Prize. She was also well known for her writings about the small-town Florida community of Cross Creek.*

SALVADOR DALI MUSEUM (Pinellas County)

The full name of the artist now known mostly by the name Dali might take up a full line of this book: Salvador Felipe Jacinto Dali I Domenech. Born in 1904 in rural Spain, he rose from those obscure beginnings to become one of the most interesting and controversial surrealist painters. In addition to his smaller paintings, this contemporary of Picasso can be remembered for his 19 large canvas paintings. Several of these are in the Dali Museum in St. Petersburg and inspire total awe when encountered. One of the authors of this book has prints of *The Hallucinogenic Toreador* and *The Discovery of America by Christopher Columbus* hanging in his house, but they do not compare to the enormous canvas on the wall of the museum. Dali was also the author of a novel and an autobiography. He fled Europe during World War II with his wife Gala, with whom he shared an unconventional relationship. His stay in the U.S. lasted only from 1940 to 1948. Before he left the continent, his work had been shown for 15 years in galleries in Spain, Paris, and other major cities. The museum was opened in St. Petersburg in 1982, seven years before Dali's death. The museum is located in downtown St. Petersburg near Bayshore Drive.

ZORA NEALE HURSTON NATIONAL MUSEUM OF THE FINE ARTS
(The Hurston Museum) (St. Lucie County)

Zora Neale Hurston grew up in Eatonville, the nation's first incorporated African-American municipality. This small, all-black community shaped young Zora, as she eavesdropped on local front-porch gossip, a familiar setting in much of her writings. Upon her mother's death, the teenager floundered in life, moving frequently around the east coast. A sympathetic Baltimore employer helped Zora enroll in high school, and many biographers believe this was when the 26 year old changed her age to 16. Three years after graduating, Zora pzublished her first short story in 1921. Heading to New York City, she studied anthropology at Barnard College and joined a new cultural movement among African-American artists, the so-called "Harlem Renaissance." Combining her scholastic field research with the movement, she wrote some of the finest African-heritage literature ever published. Some years later, embroiled in scandal and holding political views unpopular with the African-American community, Zora silently slipped from favor. Poor and never achieving national acclaim, she returned to Florida where she died January 28, 1960, at the St. Lucie County Welfare Home. From I-4 north of Orlando, take Lee Road/SR-423. Turn left on Wymore Road (first light off I-4). Take Wymore to Kennedy Boulevard and turn right. Proceed approximately one quarter mile.

"THEIR EYES WERE WATCHING GOD"

The title of this sidebar is from the classic novel of Zora Neale Hurston that describes the September hurricane that released Lake Okeechobee's deadliest floodwaters. Janie Crawford and Tea Cake's efforts to survive the storm are detailed. As the great hurricane approaches, workers in the Everglades look skyward for their eyes are watching for God to save them. With a friend, the couple abandons their home. They are pursued by on-rushing waters. They wade through waist-deep water. They shelter in a house on high ground but abandon it when floodwaters threaten it. Swimming, Janie takes hold of the first thing she can grab but is swept away from Tea Cake. She takes hold of a floating platform, on which there is a large angry dog. Tea Cake struggles to reach her, and a death struggle ensues between him and the dog. After the storm, Tea Cake is forced into labor to bury the dead. White bodies must

⋀ *Coffins piled up along the bank of a canal in Belle Glade after the terrible hurricane of 1928.*

be identified to be placed in coffins, while people of color go into a pit of quick lime. Tea Cake takes ill, for the dog he killed was rabid.

Nora Hurston wrote several other books including an autobiographical work, *Dust Tracks on the Road, Jonah's Gourd Vine, Tell My Horse,* and *Mules and Men.* Perhaps her most ambitious, and at the time controversial, novel was *Seraph on the Suwannee* in which she wrote about white characters, Florida Crackers Jim Meserve, a dominating husband, and Arvay Henson, a religious wife prone to hysterical fits.

⋏ *A scene from one of the many Tarzan movies filmed in Florida.*

In the early days of Hollywood, it was not always possible to travel to exotic locations for a movie set. Florida was an economical exotic set compared to say Africa. One example of a producer who had an "inspiration" (his company was named Inspiration Productions) to cut expenses (while sparing no quality of scenery) was Henry King. King found an exotic location on Rocky Point Island in Tampa for his early talkie, *Hell Harbor*, shot in 1930.

King needed a Caribbean setting and used Rocky Point, a spit of peninsula laden with bent over palms and a rocky shoreline on Tampa Bay. The movie centers on the descendants of Sir Henry Morgan, all pirates existing on a remote Island in the Caribbean, where violence was the order of the day—a wild film even by the lax standards of the neophyte days of yet non-existing movie codes.

Here's the plot. Morgan's great-great grandson (also named Henry Morgan) and played by Gibson Gowland, is bent on lavishing himself with gold, while sacrificing his daughter, Anita (played by Lupe Valez), into marriage to a bloodthirsty moneylender, Joseph Horngold (played by Jean Hersholt). The hero is an American sailor, Bob Wade, played by John Holland, who encounters a hornet's nest of agitated pirates as he attempts to rescue the Spanish damsel, the beautiful Lupe Velez.

The movie proved to be a good fit for the city fathers of Tampa and Hollywood. A quote from a flier of the time stated, "for more than ten weeks every imaginable courtesy and kindness was shown us by the people of Tampa, who had no other purpose than their inherent desire to make us happy." Hell Harbor is occasionally shown at the historic Tampa Theater, Tampa's answer to Atlanta's Fox Theater. The restored movie palace makes for a great venue for this obscure film. Other movies filmed in the Tampa Bay area include *Beneath the Twelve Mile Reef"* (1953) starring Robert Wagner and Terry Moore; *Sunday Dinner for A Sailor* (1944) starring Anna Baxter and John Hodiak; *Cocoon* (1985) starring Hume Crone, Don Ameche, and Jack Gilford; *H.E.A.L.T.H.* (1980) starring Carol Burnett, Dick Cavett, and James Garner; *Summer Rental* (1985) starring John Candy and Karen Austin; and *Bang the Drum Slowly* (1973) starring Michael Moriarty and Robert DeNiro. More movies filmed in Florida are listed below.

A MIGHTY WIND: THE TAMPA THEATRE'S WURLITZER

In the early 20th century, almost 7000 pipe organs were installed in theaters across America, a majority of them bearing the name of The Rudolph Wurlitzer Company. Today, The Tampa Theatre's Mighty Wurlitzer is one of less than three-dozen in use. This opulent 3-manual, 14-rank theatre organ (with nearly 1,400 pipes) is regularly featured and lovingly cared for by the Central Florida Theater Organ Society.

⋏ *The mighty Wurlitzer organ in concert at the Tampa Theater.*

POLK THEATER (Polk County)

Constructed in 1928 as an Italian Renaissance-themed retail-and-office complex anchored by a palatial movie palace, the Polk Theatre remains a Lakeland gem. Although the façade of the four-story building captures attention, the real beauty of the Polk lies within. Featuring terrazzo floors and luxurious Italian tile, a Mediterranean atmosphere dominates the theatre's interior. Rich blue ceilings with clouds and twinkling stars accent the open-air feel. In addition to the theatre's technologically advanced air-conditioning and sound systems, folks flocked to see live performances, from the likes of Tommy Dorsey, Gene Autry and Elvis Presley. However, like many movie houses and vaudeville venues throughout mid-twentieth century America, the Polk's guests marveled at a new invention invading living rooms: television. As the attendance fell, so did the Polk. Facing demolition, the theatre was purchased in 1982 by a citizens group determined to save the Polk. Now listed in the National Register of Historic Places, significant restoration of the majestic Polk was completed in 1999. Today, the theatre features live performances, films, and is available for private use. From I-4: Exit 18 South. Cross Memorial Blvd to 37 South (South Florida Ave). The Polk Theatre is located 2 miles down on the right-hand side. Parking is available in lots around theatre.

THE TAMPA THEATER (Hillsborough County)

When The Tampa Theatre opened in 1926, it was the area's first air-conditioned commercial building. Considered one of America's most lavish theaters, its Old World setting mixes English Tudor, Greek Revival, and Baroque themes with a Mediterranean courtyard lavished with flowers, statues, and even gargoyles! Through the 1960s and the early 70s, rising operation costs and dwindling attendance forced the closing of Tampa's cultural centerpiece. Faced with demolition in 1973, citizen groups urged city leaders to intervene. Five years later, the Tampa Theatre reopened, securing its place on the National Register of Historic Places. Today, the Arts Council of Hillsborough and the Tampa Theatre Foundation manage the city's only not-for-profit theater, which hosts over 600 events annually including daily screenings of first-run and independent films. From I-275 Northbound take I-275 to Exit 44. Follow Ashley Dr. to Zack Street. Turn left onto Zack Street. Follow Zack Street two blocks to Franklin Street. The Tampa Theatre is on the left-hand side.

UNIVERSAL ORLANDO THEME PARK AND HARRY POTTER WORLD

(Orange County)

Universal Studios Florida opened in 1990 with the theme that visitors could ride the movies. Rides were modeled on such blockbusters as "Back to the Future" and "ET," with soaring bicycling through the sky and under the full moon. In 1999, Islands of Adventure opened to add to the fun and thrills. In 2010, muggles all over the world were thrilled when Harry Potter World opened. Universal Resorts is second only to Disney in size and the Universal complex is a powerful draw contributing to the state's tourist revenues. It is hard to compute the current size of tourism in the state's economy, although estimates abound. It is widely believed that direct tourism, and indirect expenses like dining, travel, gifts, and other expenditures associated with tourist exceeds $100 billion dollars for the state's economy in some years, and the figure appears destined to grow. From I-4 west of Orlando, take Exit 74B, which is clearly marked with signs announcing Universal Studios. Follow the signs to Universal Boulevard and onto Hollywood Way.

THE CREEPER

From the 1930 movie *Hell's Harbor*, which was filmed in Tampa, emerged an obscure actor who rose from a bit part to become a shadowy horror-film character known as "The Creeper." Tampa resident Rondo K. Hatton was wrongly believed disfigured by mustard gas during World War I. Actually, he suffered from acromegaly, an adult disease causing progressive disfigurement of the face and limbs. In 1936, Hatton was lured to Hollywood. Voted the handsomest boy in high school, Hatton appeared as the hunchback in the title role in RKO's *Hunchback of Notre Dame*. In 1944, he played the role of Hoxton Creeper in the Sherlock Holmes' feature, *The Pearl of Death*. Before his untimely death in 1946, he played several subsequent roles as "The Creeper" in feature films.

FLORIDA'S MOVIES

Here is just a partial list of famed films made in the Sunshine State.

12 O'clock High (1944), Eglin Air Force Base

A Dolphin's Tale (2011), Clearwater

Absence of Malice (1981), Miami

Ace Ventura: Pet Detective (1933), Miami

Adaptation (2003), Naples

Airport 77 (1977), Tallahassee

Any Given Sunday (1999), Ft. Lauderdale/Miami

Apollo 13 (1995), Cape Canaveral Area

Armageddon (1993), Cape Canaveral Area

Bad Boys (1995), Miami

Bad Boys II (2002), Miami

The Bellboy (1960), Miami Beach

Beneath the 12-Mile Reef (1953), Tarpon Springs

The Birdcage, (1995), Miami Beach

Blood and Wine (1996), Key Largo

Body Heat (1981), Delray Beach, approximately Hollywood, and Lake Worth

Cadyshack (1980), Boca Raton, Davie, and Ft. Lauderdale

Cape Fear (1991), Ft. Lauderdale and Palm Beach

Cocoon (1985), St. Petersburg

Creature from the Black Lagoon (1954), Silver and Wakulla Springs

The Creature Walks Among Us (1956), Ft. Myers

Cuba Crossing (1946), Key West

Days of Thunder (1960), Daytona Beach

Distant Drums (1951), Silver Springs

Doc Hollywood (1990), Micanopy and Ocala

Donnie Brasco (1996), Ft. Lauderdale and Palm Beach

Easy to Love (1953), Cypress Gardens

Edward Scissorhands (1990), Dade City, Lakeland, Lutz, and Wesley Chapel

Follow That Dream (1962), along the Gulf Nature Coast

Frogs (1972), Wewahitcka

G. I. Jane (1997), Green Cove Springs and Jacksonville

Great Expectations (1998), Cortez and Sarasota

The Greatest Show on Earth (1952), Sarasota

The Hawk is Dying (2004), Gainesville

Hell's Harbor (1930), Tampa

Hoot (2006), Boca Grande and Ft. Lauderdale

Jaws 2 (1978), Destin and Navarre

Jaws 3-D (1983), Orlando

Key Largo (1948), Key Largo

Larry the Cable Guy: Health Inspector (2006), Orlando

Lethal Weapon 3 (1992), Orlando

License to Kill (1989), The Keys

Manhunter (1985), Captiva and Clearwater

Midnight Cowboy (1969), Miami

Midway (1976), Pensacola

Monster (2002), Orlando

Moonraker (1979), Ocala and Silver Springs

My Girl (1991), Bartow and Orlando

Never Say Never Again (1983), Silver Springs

Neptune's Darling (1955), Silver Springs

The New Adventures of Pippi Longstocking (1988), Amelia Island and Fernandina Beach

Oceans 11 (2001), St. Petersburg

Office Space (1999), Key West

Out of Time (2003), Boca Grande, Cortez, and Miami Beach

Parenthood (1989), Orlando

Passenger 57 (1992), Sanford

Porky's (1982), Ft. Lauderdale and Miami

Problem Child 2 (1990), Orlando

The Punisher (2004), Dunedin and Tampa

Rebel Without a Cause (1955), Silver Springs

Revenge of the Creature (1955), Marineland and Silver Springs

Rosewood (1997), Cedar Key and Eustis

Scarface (1983), Miami

Smokey and the Bandit 3 (1983), Ocala

Space Cowboys (2000), Cape Canaveral, Merritt Island, Titusville

Speed 2 (1997), Key West and Miami

Striptease, (1996)

Summer Rental (1985), Mediera Beach

Sunshine State (2003), Amelia Island

Tarzan's Secret Treasure (1941), Wakulla Springs

There's Something About Mary (1998), Ft. Lauderdale/Miami

Thirty Seconds Over Tokyo (1944), Eglin Air Force Base

True Lies (1994), the Keys and Miami

The Truman Show (1998), Seaside

Ulee's Gold (1996), Tallahassee

Waterboy (1998), Orlando and Palm Beach

Where the Boy's Are (1960), Ft. Lauderdale

Winds Across the Everglades (1958), Chokoloskee

Winter's Tale (2011), Clearwater

Wrestling Ernest Hemingway (1993), Ft Lauderdale

Where the Boys Are (1960), Ft Lauderdale

The Yearling (1947), Hawthorne and Ocala

Various Television Shows filmed in FL: *Flipper, Gentle Ben, Sea Hunt, Jackie Gleason Show.* For many years, the Miss Universe Contest took place in Miami Beach and was televised to the nation.

OTHER SITES AND HISTORICAL MUSEUMS

AMELIA ISLAND MUSEUM (Nassau County)

The first spoken-history museum in the state carries on the tradition with walking tours and docent tours. The museum contains information on early Native Americans, including a Timucuan village, local personalities, the Civil War, Spanish missions, and local industry. Fittingly, the musuem is located in the historic Nassau County Jail on Fernandina Beach. Visiting this museum would tie in well with Fort Clinch State Park. One arrives in quaint Fernandina by exiting I-95 west on US-A1A/SR -220 south of the Georgia border. When the road deadends on the north of Amelia Island, the museum will be close at hand.

COLLIER COUNTY NAPLES MUSEUM (Collier County)

Collier County has an exceptional museum program with the center at the 5-acre gardens at the County Government Center in Naples. There are also remote locations: a depot museum in Naples at 5th Avenue and 10th Street; an Immokalee Pioneer Museum at 1215 Roberts Avenue in Immokalee; and, an Everglades Musuem at 105 West Broadway in Everglades City. Contacts for the three museums (not the depot) are in Appendix A. Collier County is named for Barron Collier, a wealthy entrepreneur, who once owned a substantial amount of land in the county, but (more importantly) was responsible for the completion of the Tamiami Trail. Much information about Collier is available at these excellent museums. Naples lies south of Ft. Myers and can be accessed from I-75. For Everglades City, exit I-75 on SR-29 going south on I-75. Immokalee lies north of I-75 on SR-29.

FLORIDA KEYS HISTORY OF DIVING MUSEUM (Monroe County)

It is fitting that a diving museum be located in the Keys. With its beautiful coral reefs, the Keys are a magnet for diving enthusiasts from all over the world. At the museum, the visitor can follow the development of diving over 4,000 years of diving history, from early breath holders through modern-day SCUBA. Diving helmets from around the world are display in the unique "Parade of Nations" exhibit. The museum is located on the "bay side" of Overseas Highway in Islamorada, a town roughly equally distant from Miami and Key West. Hint: "bay side" means west.

FLORIDA MUSEUM OF NATURAL HISTORY (Alachua County)

Located in Gainesville, on the University of Florida campus, the Florida Museum of Natural History is the state's official, and the southeast's largest, natural history museum. The museum features exhibits on the flora, fauna, and indigenous peoples of Florida, the Southeastern U.S., and the Caribbean. In addition to their world-spanning collections and research programs, the museum features the largest North American collection of West Indies pre-Columbian artifacts. During its more than 100 years of operation, the museum has grown to house rainforests, one of the worlds largest butterfly and moth collections, and many other award-winning exhibits. From I-75, exit east on Archer (SR-24) Road. Turn left on SW 34th Street, which is SR-121. Turn right at Hull Road. The University of Florida Cultural Plaza entrance is on the right.

HERNANDO HISTORICAL MUSEUM (Hernando County)

This heritage museum is housed within a Victorian mansion. It contains over 11,000 artifacts and organizes an annual Civil War renactment of the Brooksville Raid. There are docent-guided tours during limited open hours so it best to check on hours and availability before visiting. The renactment takes place in January. From I-75 north of Tampa, take the US-301 exit west and proceed on SR-98/50 for 8 miles. Continue on Alternate-50 when SR-50 turns left. The Victorian house holding the museum stands out. It is located at 601 Museum Court.

HISTORICAL MUSEUM OF SOUTHERN FLORIDA (Dade County)

This is a large and valuable museum that dates back to 1940. Its collections include over 6,000 bound volumes, 1,900 maps, 1.5 million photographs, and 12,000 artifacts. Included in its archives are a double elephant folio edition of Audubon's The Birds of America. Although the emphasis is on South Florida and the Caribbean, materials in the musuem touch on every phase of Florida history. Within the museum's 40,000 square feet, are permanent and changing exhibits. Future and current exhibits are described online, and in fact there are online exhibits. Going south on I-95, take exit 3B, make a left on NW 2d Street and a right on NW 2d Avenue.

LIGHTNER MUSEUM (St. Johns County)

The Lightner Museum is housed in the former Alcazar Hotel, built by Henry Flager. Alcazar means palace and castle in Spanish and is itself derived from the Arabic "al qasr." It is located in St. Augustine where the historical sites lie wonderfully close and are exceedingly worthwhile to visit. The Chicago Publisher Otto Lightner purchased the hotel in 1946 to house his collection of Victorian items. Mr. Lightner graciously donated the museum to the city of St. Augustine. Across from the Ponce de Leon Hotel on King Street in downtown St. Augustine, it provides not only a look into Florida history but into the history of the world.

⩔ Lightner Museum.

MUSEUM OF FLORIDA HISTORY

(Leon County)

The official state-history museum presents Florida history through a wide range of permanent exhibits, such as "Florida's First People" and "Florida in the Civil War," a citrus packing house, and "Florida Remembers World War II." The museum hosts temporary exhibits three to four times a year. The museum is located in the R. A. Gray Building in downtown Tallahassee at 500 South Bronough Street.

MUSEUM OF SCIENCE AND INDUSTRY

(Hillsborough County)

Known locally by the affectionate acronym "MOSI," like "mosey along," the museum is a popular attraction and source of learning. Its changing exhibits have ranged from prehistory to human bodies. Within its spacious walls, permanent exhibits on Florida weather, industry, and the environment have excited children and elders. In addition to the informative and exceptional exhibits, MOSI has an large-format IMAX, capable of placing images on walls as tall as three-story buildings. The "IMAX Experience" can be overwhelming. Not only does the IMAX show scientific and educational films, it also shows first-run movies in this exciting dimension. If there were only the IMAX, a visit would be compelling. But with the world-class exhibits, no visitor or Floridan should stay away. Visit long and often, Spock. The museum is located on Fowler Avenue across the street from the University of South Florida. Fowler Avenue is an east exit of I-275 in Tampa and a west exit of I-75. MOSI lies about an equal distance from the two interstate highways.

ORANGE COUNTY REGIONAL HISTORY CENTER (Orange County)

The first-class organization covers 12,000 years of Florida history in its permanent and current exhibits. There are three floors of permanent exhibits: Florida's first peoples thru aviation; tourism before Disney and Disney World; and displays on agricultural, citrus, and the cattle industries. There are over 12,000 photographs and postcards in the archives. The center is located at 65 East Central Boulevard in Orlando. From I-4 in Orlando, exit on 83A (Amelia Street) toward downtown. Go right from Amelia Street onto Orange Avenue, then turn left at Central.

PENSACOLA HISTORICAL MUSEUM

(Escambia County)

Two floors of exhibits await the visitor with a focus on Pensacola's extensive history. The first floor exhibits change every four to six months. The second floor has permanent galleries dedicated to: Army/Navy, Martime, Multicultural, Native American, Forts and Civil War history. Outside the museum is a Haunted House Walking Tour and an Historic Trolley Tour. From I-10, exit south on I-110. Take Exit 1C onto Garden Street. Turn left at the first light to Church Street and the parking should be evident. Bayfront Parkway skirts the water and Zaragosa is a parallel street farther inland.

POLK COUNTY HISTORICAL MUSEUM

(Polk County)

Polk County is named for the 11th President of the U.S., James Polk. The town of Bartow takes its name, however, from the first general to die in the Civil War, a Confederate General named Francis Bartow. The museum's older artifacts include fossils, projectile points, and a dugout canoe, but the entire span of Polk County's history is represented. The museum is located in Old Polk County Courthouse, an impressive structure that reached 100 years of age in 2009. SR-60 passes through Bartow, and the courthouse is at 100 East Main Street. SR-60 is a west exit of The Florida Turnpike at Yeehaw Junction and an east exit of I-75 in Brandon south of Tampa.

SAFETY HARBOR MUSEUM OF REGIONAL HISTORY (Pinellas County)

Under a canopy of oak trees, Safety Harbor Museum of Regional History rests on the site of a former Tocobaga shell mound overlooking Tampa Bay. The Pre-Historic Gallery traces Florida's history from the Paleo-Indian period with fossilized remains, along with tools used by Florida's first human inhabitants, up to the 1500s. The Heritage Gallery has displays dedicated to the area's pioneers, settlers, and settler life. Included is Safety Harbor's Odet Philippe, who is considered the father of Florida grapefruit. In the Rotating Exhibit Area, temporary exhibits have celebrated various historical topics, such as the Seminoles, the Tele-Communication Industry, and the History of Baseball in the Tampa Bay area. The museum also owns the Powell Collection, one of the most comprehensive collections of Pre-Columbian artifacts from the Mississippian Culture. The museum is located at 329 Bayshore Boulevard South in Safety Harbor, a town located east of Clearwater that sits on the west side of Tampa Bay. From US-19 in northern Clearwater, SR-590 and SR-576 lead east to Safety Harbor.

ST. PETERSBURG MUSEUM OF HISTORY (Pinellas County)

This is the city's oldest museum and the third-oldest historical museum in Florida. Since 1922, it has grown so that it is presently home to a collection of over 32,000 objects of local, regional, and national interest. The signature exhibit is a working, full-size replica of a Benoist aircraft that made history as the "World's First Scheduled Commerical Airline on January 1, 1914, piloted by Tony Jannus (see account on page). Long-time residents can relive the fun of visiting Webb's City, "The World's Largest Drug Store." Webb's City sold practically everything from hardware to haircuts from 1925-1979 in a complex covering seven city blocks. James Earl "Doc" Webb's motto was "stack it high and sell it cheap." Among his gimmicks were dancing chickens and dollar bills sold for 95 cents. Webb's City attracted nearly 60,000 customers daily, many of whom came to see "the talking mermaids." The 1926 Million Dollar Pier was demolished in 1967 and replaced with the current structure. The museum is located on the approach to the present pier complex. The Million Dollar Pier was a grand building in a Mediterranean-revival style featuring a rooftop dancefloor and, of course, fishing. In a time when sharks were plentiful and loathed, the carcasses of enormous sharks hanging from hooks amazed tourists and young Florida boys. From I-275 in St. Petersburg, take I-375 downtown. Some manuerving toward the water is necessary because of one-way traffic on several roads. The Pier entrance and the museum are located three blocks north from Central Avenue on Second Avenue Northeast.

SILVER RIVER MUSEUM AND ENVIRONMENTAL EDUCATION CENTER

(Marion County)

The museum is within Silver River State Park and part of the county school system; therefore, it is closed to the public when school is in session, but open on weekends and for open houses. There are many wonderful exhibits and artifacts, but over-shadowing everything is a mammoth skeleton and the full-size skeleton of a Pleistocene short-faced bear. Silver River State Park is located one mile down CR-35 reached from SR-40 in the town of Silver Springs east of Ocala. SR-40 is an exit from I-75 in the west and I-95 in the east.

A *Cypress trees near freshwater wetlands are a familiar sight in most of Florida.*

SOUTH FLORIDA MUSEUM (Manatee County)

The museum was founded in 1946 with an extensive collection of early Native-American artifacts and materials and located at the Bradenton Memorial Pier. Twenty years later, the museum moved to its present location and added the Bishop Planetarium. A Spanish Plaza was added in 1980, followed by the Parker Manatee Aquarium in 1993. Following a 2001 electrical fire, the planetarium was rebuilt and the museum extensively remodeled. In addition to its historical displays and manatees, the Bishop Planetarium is known for spectacular light shows. From I-75 south of Tampa and north of Sarasota, exit west on SR-64 and proceed downtown, a distance of approximately 7 miles. In Bradenton, turn right on 10th Street West. The museum is on the right in two blocks.

SOUTHWEST FLORIDA MUSUEM OF HISTORY (Lee County)

The museum has artifacts and displays that are multi-era. The range includes Paleo-Indians, early Native Americans, information on local early industries, such as fishing and cattle ranching, the military fort of Fort Myers, including a replica of a Cracker house and a Pullman Car. In the cooler months, a walking historical tour supplements the museum tour. The museum also offers escorted day trips and evening events. The museum is located in downtown Fort Myers. From I-75, exit west on at Exit 138 and proceed downtown. Turn south on Jackson Street and the museum should be evident.

TAMPA BAY HISTORY CENTER
(Hillsborough County)

Located on the Hillsborough River in the Channelside District of Tampa, the Tampa Bay History Center is a valuable experience made more informative through many interactive displays, including zooming maps of the area that respond to touch and a virtual trip down the Hillsborough River of old while astride a rowing machine. The visitor can walk through an old cigar store selling such brands as Have-a-Tampa and watch movies on Florida's first peoples, the cigar industry, and the Florida Seminoles. The museum is home to The J. Thomas and Lavinia W. Touchton Collection of Florida Cartography and includes displays of maps from bygone eras that are absolutely fascinating. Other treats include information on Florida Crackers (including a replica home), items from World War II, and information on the individuals and families that contributed to Tampa's heritage. From I-275 in Tampa, exit at the Downtown Exit and follow the signs to Channelside and/or The Florida Aquarium. Water Street is a southerly turn off Channelside Drive. The museum is located on the southeast corner. The museum has parking, but when full there are a number of parking garages in the area. The chance of free parking along the streets is fairly minimal in this area which can be busy with hockey games, concerts, cruises, and nightlife.

APPENDIX

BEFORE A VISIT

Before visiting any of the locations in this book, visitors are encouraged to check with each location for hours of operations and fees. Hours of operation change, as do fees, and even area codes and email addresses change.

FLORIDA STATE PARK WEBSITE

For the many Florida parks within this appendix, the website www.myflorida.com has been used because at various times the state government has expressed (once upon a time) hopes to change all Florida activities over to one easy-to-remember website. However, at present, the reader may get more rapid access to park information by using www.floridastateparks.

Addison Blockhouse Historic State Park
2095 North Beach Street
Ormond Beach FL 32174
386-676-4-050
www.myflorida.com

Ah-Tah-Thi-Ky Museum
HC-61 Box 21-A
Clewiston FL 33440
863-902-1113
www.seminoletribe.com/museum

Alfred B. Maclay Gardens State Park
3540 Thomasville Road
Tallahassee FL 32309
850-245-2157
www.floridastateparks.org

Amelia Island Museum of History
233 South Third Street
Fernandina Beach FL 32034
904-261-7378
www.ameliamuseum.org

Anclote Key Lighthouse
Anclote Key State Park
Gulf Islands GeoPark
#1 Causeway Boulevard
Dunedin FL 34698
www.floridastateparks.com

Apalachicola Maritime Museum
103 Water Street
Apalachicola FL 32320
850-653-2500
www.ammfl.org

Archbold Biological Station
PO Box 2057
Lake Placid FL 33862
863-465-2571
www.archbold-station.org

The Armed Forces Military Museum
2050 34th Way North
Largo FL 33771
727-539-8371
www.armedforcesmuseum.com

Audubon House and Tropical Gardens
205 Whitehead Street
Key West FL 33040
305-294-2116
www.audubonhouse.com

Bahia Honda State Park
36850 Overseas Highway
Big Pine Key FL 33043
305-872-2353
www.floridastateparks.org

The Barnacle Historic State Park
3485 Main Highway
Coconut Grove FL 33133
305-442-6866
www.floridastateparks.org

Belleview Biltmore Hotel
23 Belleview Boulevard
Clearwater FL 33756
727-377-3000
www.belleviewbiltmore.com

Bethune-Cookman College
640 Dr. Mary McCleod Bethune Boulevard
Daytona Beach FL 32114
386-481-2000
www.cookman.edu

Bill Baggs Cape Florida State Park
1200 South Crandon Boulevard
Key Biscayne FL 33149
305-361-5811
www.floridastateparks.org

Biscayne National Park
9700 SW 328 Street
Homestead FL 33033
305-230-1144
www.nps.gov

Black Heritage Trail
Division of Historical Resources
500 South Bronough Street
Tallahassee FL 32399
850-245-6300
www.flheritage.com

Blue Spring State Park
2100 West French Avenue
Orange City FL 32763
386-775-3663
www.floridastateparks.org

Bok Tower Gardens
1151 Tower Boulevard
Lake Wales FL 33853
863-675-1408
www.boktowergardens.org

The Breakers
One South County Road
Palm Beach FL 33480
561-659-8465
www.thebreakers.com

Bulow Plantation Ruins Historic State Park
PO Box 655
Bunnell FL 32110
386-517-2084
www.floridastateparks.org

Busch Gardens
3605 East Bougainvillea Avenue
Tampa FL 33612
888-800-5447
www.buschgardens.com

Calusa Heritage Trail
Randell Research Center
13810 Waterfront Drive
Pineland FL 33945
Mailing: PO Box 608
Pineland FL 33945
239-283-2062
www.flmnh.ufl.edu/RRC

Cape Canaveral Lighthouse Foundation
PO Box 1978
Cape Canaveral FL 32920
407-494-5959
www.capecanaverallighthousefoundation.com

Cape St. George Lighthouse Society, Inc.
PO Box 915
Apalachicola FL 32329

Capitol Complex
400 South Monroe Street
Tallahassee FL 32399
850-487-1902
www.flhistoriccapitol.gov

Carabelle Lighthouse Association
PO Box 373
Carabelle FL 32322

The Casements
25 Riverside Drive
Ormond Beach FL 32176
386-676-3216
386-676-3363 (fax)
Thecasements@ormandbeach.org

Castillo de San Marcos
1 South Castillo Drive
St. Augustine FL 32084
904-829-6506
www.nps.gov

Cathedral Parish
38 Cathedral Place
St. Augustine FL 32084
www.thefirstparish.org

Cedar Key Historical Museum
Cedar Key Historical Society, Inc.
PO Box 222
Cedar Key FL 32625
352-543-5549
www.cedarkeymuseum.org

Cedar Key Museum State Park
12231 SW 166 Court
Cedar Key FL 32625
352-543-5350
www.floridastateparks.org

Cedar Keys Lighthouse
Cedar Keys National Wildlife Refuge
16450 NW 31st Place
Cheifland FL 32626
352-493-0328
www.fws.gov

Chalet Suzanne
3800 Chalet Suzanne Drive
Lake Wales FL 33859
863-676-6011
www.chaletsuzanne.com

Chestnut Street Cemetery
1 Bay Avenue
Apalachicola FL 32320
850-653-9319
www.cityofapalachicola.com

Citrus Tower and Museum
14 North US-27
Clermont FL 34771
352-394-4061
www.citrustower.com

Civil War Discovery Trail
The Civil War Preservation Trust
1156 15th Street NW Suite 900
Washington DC 20005
202-367-1861
www.civilwar.org

Collier County Naples Museum
3301 East Tamiami Trail
Naples FL 34112
239-252-8436
www.colliergov.net

Colonial Spanish Quarter Museum
City of St. Augustine
33 St. George Street
St Augustine FL 32084
904-825-6830
www.staugustinegovernment.com

Coral Gables Merrick House and Garden Museum
907 Coral Way
Coral Gables FL 33134
305-460-5361
www.coralgables.com

Constitutional Convention State Museum
200 Allen Memorial Highway
Port St. Joe FL 32456
850-229-8029
www.floridastateparks.org

Crooked River Lighthouse
(see Carabelle Lighthouse Association)

Cross Florida Greenway
8282 Southeast Highway 314
Ocala FL 34470
352-236-7143
www.dep.state.fl.us

Crystal River Archaeological State Park
3400 North Museum Point
Crystal River FL 34428
352-795-3817
www.floridastateparks.org

Cuban Heritage Trail
Division of Historical Resources
500 South Bronough Street
Tallahassee FL 32399
850-245-6300
www.flheritage.com

Dade Battlefield Historic State Park
7200 CR-630 South Battlefield Drive
Bushnell FL 33517
352-793-4781
www.floridastateparks.org

Daytona International Speedway
1800 West International Speedway Boulevard
Daytona Beach FL 32114
386-254-2700
www.daytonainternationalspeedway.com

DeBary Hall Historic Site
210 Sunrise Boulevard
DeBary FL 32713
386-668-3840
www.debaryhall.com

The Deland Museum of Art
600 N Woodland Blvd
Deland FL 32720
386-734-7697
www.delandmuseum.com

De Soto National Monument
8300 De Soto Memorial Highway
Bradenton FL 34209
Mailing: PO Box 15390
Bradenton FL 34280
941-792-0458
www.nps.gov

"Ding" Darling National Wildlife Refuge
1 Wildlife Drive
Sanibel FL 33957
239-472-1100
www.fws.gov

Disney World
1675 North Buena Vista Drive
Orlando FL 32830
407-939-6244
Disneyworld.disney.go.com

Division of Historical Resources
Florida Department of State
R. A. Gray Building
500 South Bronough Street
Tallahassee FL 32399-0250
850-487-2344

Don Cesar Hotel
3400 Gulf Boulevard
St. Petersburg Florida 33706
727-380-1881
www.loewshotels.com

Dow Museum of Historic Houses
149 Cordova Street
St. Augustine FL 32084
904-823-9722
www.dowmuseum.com

Dry Tortugas National Park
PO Box 6208
Key West FL 33041
305-242-7700
www.nps.gov

Eden Gardens State Park
PO Box 26
Port Washington FL 32454
850-231-4214
www.floridastateparks.org

Edison and Ford Winter Estates
2350 McGregor Boulevard
Fort Myers FL 33901
Mailing: PO Box 2368
Ft. Myers FL 33902
239-334-7419
www.efwefla.org

Egmont Key State Park
Gulf Islands GeoPark
#1 Causeway Boulevard
Dunedin FL 34698
727-893-2627
www.floridastateparks.org

Emerson Point Preserve
Manatee County Parks and Recreation
5801-17th Street West
Palmetto FL 34221
941-742-5927
www.mymanatee.com

EPCOT
1675 North Buena Vista Drive
Orlando FL 32830
407-939-6244
Disneyworld.disney.go.com

Everglades City Museum
105 West Broadway
Everglades City FL 34139
239-252-8436
www.colliergov.net

Everglades National Park
40001 SR-9336
Homestead FL 33034
305-242-7700
www.nps.gov

Everglades Wonder Garden
27180 Old US-41
Bonita Springs FL 34135
239-952-2591

Fairchild Tropical Botanical Gardens
10907 Old Cutler Road
Coral Gables FL 33156
305-667-1651
www.fairchildgarden.org

Fakahatchee Strand Preserve State Park
PO Box 548
Copeland FL 34137
239-695-4593
www.floridastateparks.org

Florida Agricultural and Mechanical University
1500 South Martin L. King, Jr. Boulevard
Tallahassee FL 32307
850-599-3000
www.famu.edu

Florida Gulf Coast Railroad Museum
12210-83d Street East
Parrish FL 34219
877-869-0800
www.frrm.org

Florida Historical Markers Program
Department of State
R. A. Gray Building
Tallahassee FL 32399
800-847-7278
850-245-6333
www.flheritage.com/preservation/markers

Florida Holocaust Museum
55 Fifth Street South
St. Petersburg FL 33701
727-820-0100
www.flholocaustmuseum.org

Florida Keys History of Diving Museum
82990 Overseas Highway
Islamorada FL 33036
305-664-9737
www.divingmuseum.com

Florida Keys National Wildlife Refuges
PO Box 43050
Big Pine Key FL 33043
305-872-0774
www.fws.gov

Florida Keys Reef Lighthouse Foundation, Inc.
PO Box 504442
Marathon FL 33050
www.floridalighthouses.org/reeflights

Florida Lighthouse Associaiton
15275 Collier Boulevard #201 PMB 179
Naples FL 34119
www.floridalighthouses.org

Florida Museum of Natural History
University of Florida Cultural Plaza
SW 34th Street and Hull Street
PO Box 112710
Gainesville FL 32611
352-846-2000
www.flmnh.ufl.edu

Florida Panther National Wildlife Refuge
3860 Tollgate Blvd. Suite 300
Naples FL 34114
239-353-8442
www.fws.gov

Florida Southern College
111 Lake Hollingsworth Drive
Lakeland FL 33801
863-680-4111
www.floridasouthern.edu

Florida World War II Heritage Trail
Division of Historical Resources
500 South Bronough Street
Tallahassee FL 32399
850-245-6300
www.flheritage.com

Fort Caroline National Monument
12713 Fort Caroline Road
Jacksonville FL 32205
904-641-7155
www.nps.gov

Fort Christmas Historical Park
1300 Fort Christmas Road
Christmas FL 32709
407-568-4149
www.orangecountyfl.net

Fort Clinch State Park
2601 Atlantic Blvd.
Fernandina Beach FL 32034
904-277-7274
www.floridastateparks.org

Fort Cooper State Park
3100 South Old Floral City Road
Inverness FL 34450
352-726-0315
www.floridastateparks.org

Fort Foster State Historic Site
15402 US 301 North
Thonotosassa FL 33592
813-987-6771
www.floridastateparks.org

Fort Gadsden
Apalachicola National Forest
PO Box 579
Bristol FL 32321
850-643-2282
www.fs.fed.us/r8/florida

Fort Matanzas National Monument
8635 A1A South
St. Augustine FL 32080
904-471-0116
www.nps.gov

Fort Mose Historic State Park
c/o Anastasia State Park
1340A A1A South
St. Augustine FL 32080
904-823-2232
www.floridastateparks.org

Fort Zachary Taylor Historic State Park
PO Box 6560
Key West FL 33041
305-292-6713
www.floridastateparks.org

Frank Lloyd Wright Visitor's Center
Florida Southern College
111 Lake Hollingsworth Drive
Lakeland FL 33801
863-680-4444
www.flsouthern.edu

Gamble Plantation Historic State Park
3708 Patten Avenue
Ellenton FL 34222
941-723-4536
www.floridastateparks.org

Gasparilla Island Maritime Museum
PO Box 100
Boca Grande FL 32921

Gasparilla Island State Park
PO Box 1150
Boca Grande FL 32921
941-964-0375
www.floridastateparks.org

Goodwood Museum and Garden
1600 Miccosukee Road
Tallahassee FL 32308
850-877-4202
www.goodwoodmuseum.org

Government House Museum
48 King Street
St. Augustine FL 32084
904-825-5079
www.stagustinegoverment.com

The Governor's Mansion
700 North Adams Street
Tallahassee FL 32303
850-922-4991
www.floridagovernorsmansion.com

Gulf Islands National Seashore
1801 Gulf Breeze Parkway
Gulf Breeze FL 32563
850-934-2600
www.nps.gov/guis/

Harry and Harriett Moore Cultural Center, Inc.
2180 Freedom Avenue
Mims FL 32754
321-264-6595
www.brevardparks.com

Harry P. Leu Gardens and Leu House Museum
1920 North Forest Avenue
Orlando, Florida 32803
Tele: (407) 246-2620
Fax: (407) 246-2849
www.leugardens.org

Haslam's Book Store
2025 Central Avenue
St. Petersburg FL 33713
727-822-8616
www.haslams.com

Hemmingway Home
907 Whitehead Street
Key West FL 33040
305-587-4282
www.hemmingwayhome.com

Hernando Historical Museum
Hernando Historical Museum Association
601 Museum Court
Brooksville FL 34601
352-799-0129
www.hernandohistoricalmuseumassoc.com

Heritage Village
11909 - 125th St North
Largo FL 33774
727-582-2128
www.pinellascounty.org/heritage

Henry B. Plant Museum
401 W Kennedy Blvd
Tampa FL 33606
813-254-1891
www.plantmuseum.com

Higgs Beach Cemetery
1899 White Street
Key West FL 33040

Highlands Hammock State Park
5931 Hammock Road
Sebring, FL 33872
863-386-6094
www.floridastateparks.org

Hillsboro Lighthouse Preservation Society, Inc.
PO Box 6062
Pompano Beach FL 33060
954-782-3313
www.HillsboroLighthouse.og

Historic L. B. Brown House
470 Second Avenue
Bartow FL 33830
863-534-0100
www.lbbrown.com

Historical Museum of Southern Florida
101 West Flagler Street
Miami FL 33130
305-375-1491
www.hmsf.org

Homeland Heritage Park
249 Church Avenue
Homeland FL 33847
863-534-3766
www.polk-county.net

Honeymoon Island State Park
1 Causeway Boulevard
Dunedin FL 34698
727-469-5942
www.floridastateparks.org

Indian Key Historic State Park
PO Box 1052
Islamorada FL 33036
305-664-2540
www.floridastateparks.org

Indian Temple Mound and Museum
139 Miracle Strip Parkway Southeast
Fort Walton Beach FL 32458
850-833-9595
www.fwb.org

J. N. "Ding" Darling National Wildlife Refuge
1 Wildlife Drive
Sanibel FL 33959
239-472-11100
www.fws.gov

John Gorrie Museum State Park
PO Box 267
Apalachicola FL 32320
850-653-9347
www.floridastateparks.org

The John and Mable Ringling Museum of Art
5401 Bay Shore Rd
Sarasota FL 34243
941-359-5700
www.ringling.org

John F. Kennedy Space Center
State Road 405
Kennedy Space Center FL 32899
321-867-5000
www.nasa.gov/centers/Kennedy

John Pennekamp Coral Reef State Park
PO Box 487
Key Largo FL 33037
305-451-1410
www.floridastateparks.org

Jonathan Dickinson State Park
16450 Southeast Federal Highway
Hobe Sound FL 33455
772-546-2771
www.floridastateparks.org

Jupiter Inlet Lighthouse
805 North US-1
Jupiter FL 33477
404-747-8380
www.jupiterlighthouse.org

Key West Cemetery
701 Passover Lane
Key West FL 33040
305-292-8177
www.keywest.com/cemetery.html

Key West Lighthouse Museum
938 Whitehead Street
Key West FL 33040
305-294-0012
www.kwah.com

The Kingsley Plantation
11676 Palmetto Avenue
Jacksonville FL 32226
904-251-3537
www.nps.gov

Koreshan State Park
3800 Corkscrew Road
Estero FL 33928
239-992-0311
www.floridastateparks.org

Lake Jackson Mounds Archaeological State Park
3600 Indian Mounds Road
Tallahassee FL 32303
850-922-6007
www.floridastateparks.org

Letchworth-Love Mounds Archaeologial State Park
4500 Sunray Road South
Tallahassee FL 32309
850-922-6007
www.floridastateparks.org

L. B. Brown House
(see Historic L. B. Brown House)

Lightner Museum
75 King Street
St. Augustine FL 32084
904-824-2874
www.lightnermuseum.org

Madira Bickel Mound State Archaeological Site
3708 Patten Avenue
Ellenton FL 34222
941-723-4536
www.floridastateparks.org

Mandarin Community Club, Inc.
12447 Mandarin Road
Mandarin FL 32223
904-268-1622

Marie Selby Botanical Gardens
811 South Palm Avenue
Sarasota FL 34236
941-366-5731
www.selby.org

Marineland
9600 Oceanshore Boulevard
St. Augustine FL 32080
904-471-1111
www.marineland.net

Marjorie Kinnan Rawlings Historic State Park
18700 South CR-325
Hawthorne FL 32640
352-466-3672
www.floridastateparks.org

Memorial Presbyterian Church
32 Sevilla Street
St. Augustine FL 32084
904-829-6451
www.memorialpcusa.org

Micanopy Historical Society Museum
PO Box 462
Micanopy FL 32667
352-466-3200
www.afn.org/micanopy

Mission de Nombre de Dios
27 Ocean Avenue
St. Augustine FL 32084
904-828-2809
www.missionsandshrines.org

Mission San Luis
2100 West Tennessee Street
Tallahassee FL 32304
850-487-3711
www.missionsanluis.org

Monastery of St. Bernard
16711 West Dixie Highway
North Miami Beach FL 33160
305-945-1461
www.spanishmonastery.com

Morikami Museum and Japanese Gardens
4000 Morikami Park Road
Delray Beach FL 33446
561-966-6000
www.morikami.org

Mound Key State Archaeological Park
(contact Koreshan State Park)

Mount Zion Baptist Church
301 NW 9th Street
Miami FL 33136
305-379-4147

Museum of Florida History
R. A. Gray Building
500 South Bronough Street
Tallahassee FL 32399
850-245-6400
www.museumoffloridahistory.com

Museum of Science and Industry
4800 East Fowler Avenue
Tampa FL 33617
813-987-6100
www.mosi.org

National Key Deer Refuge
28950 Watson Boulevard
Big Pine Key FL 33043
305-872-0774
www.fws.gov

Natural Bridge Battlefield Historic State Park
7502 Natural Bridge Road
Tallahassee FL 32305
850-922-6007
www.floridastateparks.org

Neily Trappman Studio
(By appointment only)
5409 21st Avenue South
Gulfport FL 33707
www.floridafrontier.org

Office of the Greenways
Cross Florida Greenway
Ocala Field Office
8282 SE Highway 314
Ocala FL 34470
352-236-7143
352-236-9121 (fax)
www.myflorida.com

Old Fort Lauderdale Village and Museum
219 SW Second Avenue
Fort Lauderdale FL 33301
954-463-4431

Oldest House Museum Complex
14 Sr. Francis Street
St. Augustine FL 32084
904-824-2872
www.staugustinehistoricalsociety.org

Olustee Battlefield Historic State Park
PO Box 40
Olustee FL 32072
386-758-0400
www.floridastateparks.org

Orange County Regional History Center
65 East Central Boulevard
Orlando FL 32803
407-836-8510
www.thehistorycenter.org

Panama Canal Museum
7985 13th Street #100
Seminole FL 33772
727-394-9338
www.panamacanalmuseum.org

Paynes Creek Historic State Park
888 Lake Branch Road
Bowling Green FL 33834
863-375-4717
www.myflorida.com

Paynes Prairie Preserve State Park
100 Savannah Boulevard
Micanopy FL 32667
352-466-3397
www.floridastateparks.org

Pena-Peck House
143 St. George Street
St. Augustine FL 32084
904-829-5064
www.staugustinewomans-exchange.com

Pennekamp (see John Pennkeamp)

Pensacola Historic District/Seville Square
Pensacola Chamber of Commerce
1401 East Gregory Street
Pensacola FL 33250
850-874-1234
www.VisitPenscaola.com

Pensacola Historical Museum
115 East Zaragosa Street
Pensacola FL 32502
850-595-1559
www.pensacolahistory.org

Pensacola Naval Air Station
190 Radford Boulevard
Pensacola FL 32508

Philippe Park
2525 Philippe Parkway
Safety Harbor FL 34695
727-669-1947
www.pinellascounty.org/park/11_Philippe

Polk County Historical Museum
100 East Main Street
Bartow FL 33830
863-534-4386
www.polk-county.net

Polk Theatre
127 South Florida Avenue
Lakeland, Florida 33801
Phone: (863)-682-7553
www.polktheatre.org

Ponce de Leon Hotel
74 King Street
St. Augustine FL 32084
www.flagler.edu

Ponce de Leon Inlet Lighthouse Museum
4931 South Peninsula Drive
Ponce Inlet FL 32127
386-761-1821
www.ponceinlet.org

Willie C. Regan
Story Art Studio
5686 41st Street
Vero Beach FL 32967
772-562-6742
www.highwayman-wcregan,com

Ringling Museum
(see John and Mable Ringling Museum of Art)

Safety Harbor Museum of Regional History
329 South Bay Shore Boulevard
Safety Harbor FL 34695
727-726-1668
www.safetyharbormuseum.org

Saint Augustine Alligator Farm, Inc.
999 Anastasia Boulevard
St. Augustine FL 32080
904-824-3337
www.alligatorfarm.com

Saint Augustine Lighthouse and Museum
81 Lighthouse Avenue
St. Augustine FL 32084
904-829-0745
www.stauglight.com

Saint George Episcopal Church
10560 Fort George Road
Fort George Island FL 32226
904-251-9272
www.saintgeorgechurch.us

Saint George Island State Park
1900 East Gulf Beach Avenue
St. George FL 32338
850-927-2111
www.floridastateparks.org

Saint George Lighthouse Association
201 Bradford Street
St. George Island FL 32328
850-927-2972

Saint Marks Lighthouse
Saint Marks National Wildlife Refuge
Box 68
St. Marks FL 32355
850-925-6121
www.fws.org

Saint Petersburg Museum of History
335 Second Avenue Northeast
St. Petersburg FL 33701
727-894-1052
www.spmoh.org

Salvador Dali Museum
One Dali Boulevard Southeast
727-823-3767
www.thedali.org

San Marcos de Apalachee Historic State Park
148 Old Fort Road
St. Marks FL 32355
850-925-6216
www.floridastateparks.org

SeaWorld Orlando
7007 SeaWorld Drive
Orlando FL 32821
888-800-5447
www.seaworld.com

Segui-Kirby Smith House
271 Charlotte Street
St. Augustine FL 32084
904-824-2872
www.staugustinehistoricalsociety.org

Silver River Museum
Marion County Schools
1445 NE 58th Avenue
Ocala FL 34470
352-236-5401
www.SilverRiverMuseum.com

Silver Springs State Park
1425 NE 58th Avenue
Ocala FL 34470
352-236-7148
www.floridastateparks.org

South Florida Museum
201 10th Street West
Bradenton FL 34205
941-746-4131
www.southfloridamuseum.org

Southwest Florida Museum of History
2031 Jackson Street
Ft. Myers FL 33901
239-332-5955
www.swflmuseumofhistory.com

S S Victory Mariners Memorial
705 Channelside Drive
Tampa FL 33602
813-228-8766
www.americanvictory.org

State Capitol (Historic Capitol)
400 South Monroe Street
Tallahassee FL 32399
850-487-1902
www.myflorida .com

Tampa Bay History Center
801 Old Water Street
Tampa FL 33602
813-228-0097
www.tampabayhistorycenter.org

Tampa Bay Watch Lighthouse
Tampa Bay Watch, Inc.
3000 Pinellas Bay Way South
Tierre Verde FL 33715
727-867-8166
www.TampaBayWatch.org

Tampa Theatre
711 North Franklin Street
Tampa FL 33602
813-274-8981
www.tampatheatre.org

Tarpon Springs Area Historical Society
160 East Tarpon Avenue
Tarpon Springs FL 34689
727-943-4624
tarponhistorical@verizon.net

Tarpon Springs Chamber of Commerce
11 East Orange
Tarpon Springs FL 34689
727-943-4624
www.tarponspringschamber.com

Theater of the Sea
84721 Overseas Hwy
Islamorada, FL 33036
(305) 664-2431
www.theaterofthesea.com

Timucuan Ecological and Historic Preserve
12713 Fort Caroline Road
Jacksonville FL 32225
904-641-7155
www.nps.gov

Tomoka State Park
2099 North Beach Street
Ormond Beach FL 32174
386-676-4050
www.floridastateparks.org

Tony Jannus Park
City of Tampa Parks and Recreation
3402 West Columbus Drive
Tampa FL 33607
813-274-8615
www.tampagov.net

Torreya State Park
HC-2 Box 70
Bristol FL 32321
850-643-2674
www.floridastateparks.org

Trinity Episcopal Church
215 St. George Street
St. Augustine FL 32084
904-824-2876
www.trinityepiscopalparish.org

Truman's Little White House
111 Front Street
Key West FL 33040
305-294-9911
www.trumanlittlewhitehouse.com

Union Bank Building
219 Apalachee Parkway
Tallahassee FL 32301
850-561-2603

Universal Orlando
Business Address
1000 Universal Studios Plaza
Orlando FL 32819
407-363-8000
www.universalorlando.com

Venetian Pool
2701 Desoto Boulevard
Coral Gables, FL 33134
Phone: (305) 460-5306
www.venetianpool.com

Vinoy Resort and Gulf Club
501 5ᵗʰ Avenue NE
St. Petersburg FL 32701
727-894-1000
www.marriott.com

Vizcaya Museum and Gardens
3521 South Miami Avenue
Miami FL 33129
305-250-9133
www.vizcayamuseum.org

Charles Walker
Getrude Wallker Gallery
Both at 171 Melody Lane
Fort Pierce FL 34950
772-466-8100
www.gertrudewalkergallery.com

Wakulla Springs State Park
550 Wakulla Park Dr
Wakulla Springs FL 32327
850-926-0700
www.floridastateparks.org

Walt Disney World
(See Disney World)

Washington Oaks Garden State Park
6400 North Oceanshore Boulevard
Palm Coast FL 32137
386-446-6780
www.floridastateparks.org

Weedon Island Preserve
1800 Weedon Drive NE
St. Petersburg FL 33702
727-453-6500
www.weedonislandcenter.org

Weeki Wachee Springs State Park
6131 Commercial Way
Weeki Wacheee FL 34606
352-596-5656
www.weekiwachee.com

Whitehall/Flagler Museum
One Whitehall Way
Palm Beach FL 33480
561-655-2833
www.flaglermuseum.us

Ybor City Historic District
Visitor Information Center
1600 East 8ᵗʰ Avenue
Tampa FL 33605
813-241-8838
www.ybor.org

Yulee Sugar Mill Ruins Historic State Park
3400 North Museum Pointe
Crystal River FL 34428
352-795-3817
www.floridastateparks.ogr

Zora Neale Hurston Museum
227 East Kennedy Boulevard
Eatonville FL 32745
407-647-3307
www.zoranealehurstonfestival.com

FURTHER READING

ART OF THE FLORIDA SEMINOLE AND MICCOSUKEE INDIANS, Dorothy Downs, University Press of Florida

A SACRED TRUST, Robert N. Pierce, University Press of Florida

AN AMERICAN BEACH FOR AFRICAN AMERICANS, Marsha Dean Phelts, University Press of Florida

THE AFRICAN AMERICAN HERITAGE OF FLORIDA, David R. Colburn and Jane L. Landers, editors, University Press of Florida

APALACHEE, John H. Hann, University of Florida Press

ARCHEOLOGY OF PRECOLUMBIAN FLORIDA, Jerald T. Milanich, University Press of Florida

THE BLACK SEMINOLES, Kenneth W. Porter, University Press of Florida

THE CALUSA AND THEIR LEGACY, Darcie MacMahon and William Marquardt, University Press of Florida

CRACKER TIMES AND PIONEER LIVES: THE FLORIDA REMINISCENCES OF GEORGE GILLETTE KEEN AND SARAH PAMELA WILLAMS, James M. Denham and Canter Brown, University of South Carolina Press.

THE CROSS IN THE SAND, Michael V. Gannon, University Press of Florida

DRAWN TO THE LIGHT: The History of Cape Canaveral, Sonny Witt, Central Plains Books

ECHOES FROM A DISTANT FRONTIER: THE aCORRESPONDENCE OF THE BROWN SISTERS FROM FLORIDA ANTEBELLUM FLORIDA, James M. Denham and Keith L. Huneycutt, University of South Carolina Press.

THE EVERGALDES: RIVER OF GRASS, Marjory Stoneman Douglas, Pineapple Press

FLORIDA: A SHORT HISTORY, Michael Gannon, University Press of Florida

FLORIDA'S FABULOUS LIGHTHOUSES, Tim Ohr, World Publications

FLORIDA'S COWBOYS: KEEEPERS OF THE LAST FRONTIER, Carleton Ward, Jr. University Press of Florida

FLORIDA'S FIRST PEOPLE, Robin C. Brown, Pineapple Press

FLORIDA HISTORICAL WALKING TOURS, Roberta Sandler, Pineapple Press

FLORIDA INDIANS AND THE INVASION FROM EUROPE, Jerald T. Milanich, University Press of Florida

FLORIDA'S INDIANS FROM ANCIENT TIMES TO PRESENT, Jerald T. Milanich, University Press of Florida

FLORIDA'S LIGHTOUSES IN THE CIVIL WAR, Neil Hurley, Middle River Press

FLORIDA'S MUSEUMS AND CULTURAL ATTRACTIONS, Bardon and Laurie, Pineapple Press

FLORIDA'S PAST, Gene M. Burnett, Pineapple Press

FLORIDA'S PEACE RIVER FRONTIER, Canter Brown, University Press of Florida

FLORIDA'S SEMINOLE INDIANS, Wilfred T. Neill, Great Outdoors Publishing

FLORIDA SHERIFFS: A HISTORY, 1821-1945, William W. Rogers and James M. Denham, Sentry Press

FORT MOSE, Kathleen Degean and Darcie MacMahon, University Press of Florida

FOSSILING IN FLORIDA, Mark Renz

THE FLORIDA KEYS, John Viele, Pineapple Press

HERNANDO DE SOTA AND THE INDIANS OF FLORIDA, Jerald T. Milanich, University Press of Florida

THE HISTORY OF CASTILLO DE SAN MARCOS, Luis Arana and Albert Manucy, Eastern National

INDIAN MOUNDS YOU CAN VISIT, I. Mac Perry, Great Outdoors Publishing Company

JONATHAN DICKINSON'S JOURNAL, Florida Classics Library

LEGENDS OF THE SEMINOLES, Betty Mae Jumper, Pineapple

LIES ACROSS AMERICA, Press James Lowen, The New Press

LIFE AND TRAVELS OF JOHN BARTRAM, Edmund and Dorothy Smith Berkeley, The Florida State University Press

MISSIONS TO THE CALUSA, John H. Hann, University of Florida Press

A ROGUE'S PARADISE: CRIME AND PUNISHMENT IN ANTEBELLUM FLORIDA, James M. Denham, University of Alabama Press.

SLAVERY IN FLORIDA: TERRITORIAL DAYS TO EMANCIPATION, Larry E. Rivers, University Press of Florida.

SOUTH FLORIDA FOLKLORE, Bucuvalas, Bulger, and Kennedy, University Press of Mississippi

SUNSHINE IN THE DARK, Robert Ingalls, University Press of Florida

THE NEW HISTORY OF FLORIDA, Michael Gannon, editor University Press of Florida

THE SPANISH MISSIONS OF FLORIDA, Bonnie G. McEwan (editor), University Press of Florida

THE SWAMP, Michael Grunwald, Simon & Schuster

THE TRAVELS OF WILLIAM BARTRAM, William Bartram, Yale University Press

URBAN VIGILANTES IN THE NEW SOUTH, Robert P. Ingalls, University Press of Florida

PHOTO CREDITS

Pete Carmichael (PC), Charles Walker Studio (CW), Daniel Ewert (DE), Flagler Museum (Flagler), Florida Memory (FM), Library of Congress (LC), Paul Marcellini (PM), John Moran (JM), Tim Ohr (TO), James Phillips (JP), Sanders Archive (SA), Jim Stem (JS), Neily Trappman Studio (NP), St. Petersburg Museum of History (SP), Universiy of Florida (UF).

Front cover: Flagler; Inside front cover: LC; p.1: LC; p.5, upper left: FM, upper right: UF, bottom right: JP; p.6: FM; p.8, middle right: LC; p.9, all: FM; p.10, upper left: JS, bottom right: FM; p.11, bottom left: TO; p.12, upper right: PC; p.14, upper right: JS; p.15: FM; p.16, upper right: JS, bottom right: FM; p.18, all: FM; p.21-23, all: FM; p.25, upper right: FM, middle: JS; p.26-27: JS; p.29, middle: PC, bottom left: JS; p.30, all: JS; p.31: FM; p.33-34, all: FM; p.36: TO; p.37, upper right: JP; p.38, upper: LC, bottom right: PC; p.45, bottom left: FM; p.47, upper right: FM;

p.48, upper: PM; p.49: JS; p.50, upper: SA, bottom right: JS; p.51: JS; p.52, upper left: FM; p.56, upper: FM, bottom right: JS; p.57, upper: PM; p.58, middle: FM; p.59, all: Flagler; p.60: FM; p.61: SA; p.62-63, all: FM, p.69, all: FM; p.71, middle: FM; p.72: SP; p.73, all: TO; p.74: SA; p.75, bottom right: FM; p.76: JS; p.78-80, all: FM; p.82, bottom right: FM; p.84, middle and bottom right: FM; p.85, upper right: FM; p.88: CW; p.89: JP; p.90, upper right: FM; p.91-92, all: FM; p.93: JS; IBC: JS; BC, middle left and bottom right: FM.